ATLANTIC MEETING

ATLANTIC MEETING

An Account of Mr. Churchill's Voyage in
H.M.S. *Prince of Wales*, in August, 1941,
and the Conference with President
Roosevelt which resulted in
the Atlantic Charter

by

H. V. MORTON

METHUEN

Published by Methuen in 2016

1

Methuen
Orchard House, Railway Street
Slingsby, York YO62 4AN

First published in Great Britain by
Methuen in 1943

A CIP catalogue record for this
book is available from the British Library

ISBN: 978 0 413 77791 1

Typeset by SX Composing DTP, Rayleigh, Essex
Printed and bound in Great Britain by CPI Group (UK) Ltd,
Croydon, CR0 4YY

www.methuen.co.uk

CONTENTS

ILLUSTRATIONS

When Mr. Wendell Willkie arrived in London in January 1941, he handed to Mr. Churchill a verse from Longfellow written in the President's handwriting together with Mr. Roosevelt's comment that "it applies to your people as it does to us." In August, 1941, Mr. Churchill took with him from England cards on which this verse was illuminated, and after the Atlantic Charter had been approved on August 12th, both statesmen signed the cards and each kept a copy as a souvenir of the Atlantic Meeting. The reproduction in colour is from the card in the possession of the Prime Minister

Frontispiece
(Copyright design by courtesy of Messrs. Raphael Tuck
& Sons, Ltd.)

FOREWORD

by the Rt Hon Lord Owen to reprint of
Atlantic Meeting by H.V. Morton. (Methuen, 1943)

THIS little gem of a book is an account by a brilliant writer of religious and travel books and who out of the blue is summoned to see the Minister of Information, Brendan Bracken, on Saturday xx August 1941.

"I have an extraordinary proposition to put up to you," said Bracken "I want you to leave England for three weeks, but I regret to say I can't tell you where you are going or what you will see when you get there. I can only say that if you go you will see history in the making and be present at one of the great moments of the war. Will you go?"

"Yes, of course I'll go."

Only then was Morton told he would leave London the next day and England on Monday in a battleship with the novelist, Howard Spring, and you "have been chosen to describe whatever it is you are going to see."

"It's not likely you'll hear any shooting unless Germany sends out a pocket battleship to intercept you." Told to wear the clothes he was wearing and advised to pack a dinner jacket Morton wrote "It was exciting ... like the opening of

a good Buchan spy novel." In some senses his writing up of
the next three weeks for pace of narrative, surprise and deli-
cious vignettes reads like a thriller.

Before Morton travelled up to London, speculating
where he was heading, he heard on the radio that President
Roosevelt was going on a fishing holiday up the New
England coast without the press. Instinct meant Morton
included in his luggage Baedeker's guides to 'The United
States' and 'Canada'. The latter was very useful on
Newfoundland. Joining the train at Marylebone Station it
was only when they stopped at a country station and
Winston Churchill got on the train that he realised what
was happening.

I will add nothing to the subsequent fascinating story, but
only explain why, in my judgement, based on reading
Robert Sherwood's Volume 1, page 301–365 'The White
House Papers of Harry L. Hopkins' Bracken was correct in
anticipating that Churchill's meeting with Roosevelt was
going to be "one of the great moments of the war."

On Friday 11 July 1941 in Washington, President
Roosevelt drew a line on a small map of the Atlantic
Ocean that he had torn out of the National Geographic
Magazine and gave it to Harry Hopkins. On Sunday,
Hopkins flew from Gander, Newfoundland to Prestwick,
Scotland and went straight to see Churchill and showed
him the map. The war in Russia with the invading
Germans was in its fourth week. No one knew how long
it would last, whether the Russians could defend Moscow
or even avoid defeat. Roosevelt's map (photostat included
in case you want to show it) showed the policing of the
Atlantic sea area for which the U.S. Navy would assume

responsibility in order to free up British escort ships for service elsewhere, particularly the Murmansk sea route to get supplies to the Russians. It was a profound shift of the President's position.

This was happening against a strongly held belief amongst the U.S. Chiefs of Staff that the British Empire was making too many sacrifices in trying to maintain what they saw as an indefensible position in the Middle East. Hopkins, now in London, decided that since every key decision on American production and Lend Lease depended on what was happening in Russia and information was sketchy he should make a quick trip to Moscow before Churchill and Roosevelt and their respective Chiefs met as planned at the Atlantic Conference. This he did in a new flying boat link from Invergorden to Archangel. He spoke to Stalin on arrival at some length who said "You are our guest; you have but to command" and that "he would be at his disposal every day". Hopkins ended two days in Moscow with a four hour second visit with Stalin and gained far more information than had ever been given to any outsider. He made three reports. Part III was "For The President Only." Stalin said "it would be very difficult for Britain and Russia combined to crush the German military machine. The one thing that could defeat Hitler, and perhaps without ever firing a shot, would be the announcement that the United States was going to war with Germany."

Stalin wanted Hopkins to tell the President that he would welcome the American troops on any part of the Russian front under the complete command of the American Army. Hopkins told Stalin that his "mission related entirely to matters of supply and that the matter of our joining in the war would be decided largely by Hitler himself and his encroachment upon our fundamental interests."

Hopkins then flew back to Scotland and Scapa Flow in time to come on board *HMS The Prince of Wales* with Churchill. The Prime Minister had kept all the Allied Heads of Government informed of his travel arrangements to the extent of saying that this would be his first meeting with the President. He tended to forget that he had met Roosevelt when he was Assistant Secretary of the Navy in the First World War at a banquet in London and it was something of a sore point with Roosevelt that he had apparently failed to notice the young American who remembered their meeting clearly. When they met Hopkins told friends "You'd have thought Winston was being carried up into the heavens to meet God!"

On the wording of the Atlantic Charter Churchill did not get his own way over Japan hoping for a 'mailed fist' threat and the U.S. instead reasserted its power as a sovereign nation looking after its own interests which meant nothing changed. Churchill was also embarrassed by Point Three. "They respect the right of all peoples to choose the form of Government under which they will live" (drafted by himself) because Point Four referred to "all States, great or small" and Point Five to "all nations." Not surprisingly, people in India, Burma, Malaya and Indonesia asked did it all apply to them? Roosevelt had, in effect, separated the U.S. from Churchill's post-war Imperial dreams and left the way open for Attlee's commitment to independence for India.

For Churchill, the big news reporting to his government was that he had established "warm and deep personal relations with our great friend." In Britain, there was a sense of anti-climax with no great American armada coming across the Atlantic. The all-important threshold had, however, been passed at the meetings in the one place that mattered: Roosevelt's mind.

Though he insisted to the press, party leaders and members of his Cabinet that nothing had changed, in fact, everything had changed. Best confirmed to John Colville, Churchill's Private Secretary, on 19 August – who was not there – by John Martin who was. He had heard Roosevelt say that "he did not intend to declare war: he intended to wage it." (*The Fringes of Power. Downing Street Diaries 1939–1955*).

David Owen
March 2016

INTRODUCTION

UPON Sunday, August 3rd, 1941, Mr. Winston Churchill and the Chiefs of Staff travelled by train to the North, where on the following day, and in conditions of the greatest secrecy, they embarked in a battleship. Five days later, upon Saturday, August 9th, the battleship dropped anchor in a lonely bay off the shores of Newfoundland. American warships were waiting there with President Roosevelt, who had come so secretly to the rendezvous that the entire Press of America was speculating upon his disappearance. In that desolate bay, which reminded everyone of the Hebrides, with low hills rising mistily in the grey air, the warships lay at anchor while the two statesmen conducted their conference, the published outcome of which was the Atlantic Charter.

When the Roosevelt-Churchill conference became known to the public it was called the most dramatic personal encounter of the War, and although we live in days which bring with them a succession of spectacular happenings nothing has yet occurred to rob that occasion of such a title. Indeed the march of events and America's entry into the War give to that meeting an even deeper significance, and it is safe to predict that the Atlantic conference will take its place among the great meetings in history.

So swiftly does life flow in these days that it is not easy to cast the mind back even for eighteen months and to remember what we were thinking and saying at that time, but it is possible to recollect the feeling of astonishment and pride with which the people of Great Britain learned that their indomitable leader, daring Hitler's U-boats, had crossed and re-crossed the Atlantic battleground in the prosecution of his mission. Never before in time of war had a statesman ventured so far and for so long a time into regions open to enemy attack, and Mr. Churchill, in offering Hitler a chance to take a shot at him, still further endeared himself to his countrymen and at the same time put into action a contempt for the boasts and stratagems of his enemy that he had so often and so vigorously expressed in words.

This voyage across the Atlantic at the height of the War, and the meeting far from the haunts of man of the two great leaders who, although friends, were not yet companions in arms, had that quality which commends itself to the imagination. Seen against the tremendous events of 1939–41, it will live in the history books of the future and will arouse the interest and curiosity of generations yet unborn. Men will ask what it was like to cross the Atlantic with Winston Churchill in wartime. It may be that a dramatist, an artist or a writer of films will wish to picture Churchill upon the admiral's bridge gazing through the mists of early morning towards the shores of the New World. Time may prove that such a picture was one of the great symbolic moments of the War. And should this be so, the writer and the artist will have many a question to ask. What did he wear? What did he look like? Was he well and in good spirits? Was he ill? What did he talk about? How did he spend his time as the warship carried him across the ocean? They will want to know the atmosphere of that voyage, for it was not a pleasure cruise: it was a dangerous occasion. Everyone in the ship knew that Hitler had never been offered a finer target. What then was life like in that ship? Those are some of the questions I will try to answer, but first I must describe briefly the origin of the Atlantic meeting.

On July 17th, 1941, a fleet of American bombers consigned to the R.A.F. under the Lease-Lend Act flew the Atlantic, bringing with them as passenger a slim, frail man with the heart of a lion, President Roosevelt's friend and confidant, Mr. Harry Hopkins. He had come to confer on the President's behalf with Mr. Churchill and to discuss the working of the Lease-Lend Act. Towards the end of July, on the eve of his departure by air for Moscow, Mr. Hopkins accepted an invitation, never before offered to the member of another nation, to attend a meeting of the War Cabinet at No. 10, Downing Street. After the meeting he had a private talk with the Prime Minister.

Behind No. 10, and separated from the Horseguards by a high brick wall, is an L-shaped garden where Mr. Churchill occasionally takes a walk. It is not a spectacular garden in spite of Mrs. Neville Chamberlain's earnest attempts to transform it. There is a paved terrace, some grass and a few official-looking flowers obviously blooming by arrangement with the Office of Works. Although separated by only a few yards from the Cabinet Room, where so much history has been made, no great events have ever overflowed into the garden of No. 10, which has accordingly enjoyed a smooth and uneventful career, except for one brief moment in the Nineteenth Century when an unfortunate experiment conducted on the lawn with gun cotton blew in all the windows at the back of the house. However, on that afternoon in the summer of 1941 history at last decided to alight upon that sombre lawn as Mr. Churchill, selecting a cigar, led his visitor outside for a breath of fresh air. When Mr. Churchill re-entered No. 10 he had decided to cross the Atlantic.

As the two men walked up and down the garden they discussed the problems of the War. It was a significant moment. Casting our minds back to July, 1941, we may remember that the British genius for survival seemed to have touched new heights. Dunkirk was ancient history. The Battle of Britain had been won in the daylight of the preceding summer. The long night Blitz of Britain was just beginning to slacken. For the first time for nearly twelve months the death-rate from German air raids dropped in June and July, 1941, from between five and six thousand a month into hundreds. London and our great cities, bleeding from ten months of cruel raids, were binding their wounds with courage and were with thankfulness sleeping through summer nights which were strangely and beautifully silent.

Weary as we were, we were still able to rejoice, for the Royal Air Force was hitting back at last. Our fighters were sweeping the skies of France by day, by the light of summer moons our bombers were finding targets in Germany. In Libya, those Italians not enjoying our hospitality had been chased back to their own desert by General Wavell; in Syria, our brief, melancholy fight with France had ended in an armistice signed at Acre. But these events had been overshadowed by two tremendous developments, one in the east, the other in the west. Upon June 22nd, Hitler, with a reckless love of anniversaries, for he had selected the date of Napoleon's march on Moscow, invaded Russia, and by the end of July the most violent mechanised conflict known in the history of warfare was raging along the Stalin Line from the Arctic to the Black Sea. Stalin had ordered his retreating troops to "scorch" the earth. The moment Russia was attacked Mr. Churchill, broadcasting at nine o'clock on a Sunday evening, June 22nd, hailed the Russians as allies, and announced to the world Britain's resolution to fight by Russia's side. July was only twelve days old when the Anglo-Soviet Agreement was signed in the presence of Stalin, promising aid to Russia and declaring that neither nation would make a separate peace. So much for the East.

Across the Atlantic, a new and mighty world champion was arming. The United States had passed the Lease-Lend Act and the mounting products of her war industries were to be given to the enemies of Germany, among whom Russia was now to be numbered. At the beginning of July, America took her first step towards active intervention in the War when she sent United States troops to Iceland. In the House of Commons on July 9th, Mr. Churchill said: "The military occupation of Iceland by the forces of the United States is of first rate political and strategical importance; in fact it is one of the most important things that has happened since the War began." This great event was swiftly followed by America's decision to guard the sea ways to Iceland with ships of the American Navy.

Thus it is not difficult to imagine the general trend of their conversation as Mr. Churchill and Mr. Hopkins walked up and down the modest lawn of No. 10 upon that evening in late July. That they discussed the new situation created by Hitler's attack on Russia, and the need to help Russia, goes without saying. It is also not impossible that they mentioned Japan, which at that moment was getting ready to spring. Replying to a remark of Mr. Churchill's, Mr. Hopkins said what a pity it was that he could not speak with the President face to face and bring before him, as no one else could, the mighty problems they had discussed. And how gladly, said Mr. Hopkins, the President would meet Mr. Churchill and learn from him at first hand what Britain was doing and what she hoped to do in the War. Mr. Churchill paused in his walk. He had made up his mind. He had decided to cross the Atlantic and meet President Roosevelt.

Early on the following morning the President of the United States was called to the telephone in the White House to receive a Transatlantic call. He heard the unmistakable voice of Winston Churchill proposing a meeting, and he agreed. So the Atlantic meeting was arranged.

It was decided that it should take place off the shores of Newfoundland. The President was to leave in his yacht for a fishing holiday up the New England coast and when at sea was to transfer to a warship and go escorted by naval vessels to the rendezvous. Mr. Churchill was to cross the Atlantic in the greatest possible secrecy in H.M.S. *Prince of Wales*, then our latest battleship just back from the shipyard after her conflict with the *Bismarck*.

No sooner was the decision made than it was carried out. Mr. Churchill decided to leave England on August 4th. The President left in his yacht, the *Potomac* on the 3rd. Mr. Hopkins, who had left for Moscow on July 30th to meet Stalin, arranged to fly back to Scapa Flow in time to join the *Prince of Wales* and cross the Atlantic with Mr. Churchill. Thus on the eve of the August Bank Holiday week-end which, even in wartime, most wickedly trails a certain lassitude about it, Whitehall found itself suddenly precipitated into a State secret of the utmost magnitude and importance.

An enormous amount of work had to be done in a short time. The Prime Minister, the Chiefs of Staff and their technical advisers cannot be spirited to the other side of the Atlantic without a great deal of organisation. It was necessary to place the battleship and an escort of destroyers under orders. It was necessary to charter a special train to take the party to the port of embarkation. It was necessary to order special food and other stores. Clerks, secretaries and a numerous staff of Admiralty cipher clerks had to be sent ahead to the battleship to establish their organisation. And it was essential that none of these people should have the slightest idea of what was happening or where he was going. So upon the last day of July, 1941, and the 1st of August, various departments of State tapped men on the shoulder, told them that they had been selected for "a special task" that would involve their absence from home and left it at that. And upon Monday, August 4th, the *Prince of Wales* steamed off through northern mists into the Atlantic.

It was, of course, natural that in America, a country still at peace and subject to no censorship and acutely sensitive to news, the absence of the President should have created greater comment than the absence of Mr. Churchill from London. Rumours there might be in London, and there were, but Press and wireless comment there could not be. It was otherwise in the United States. The hue and cry began as early as August 5th—Mr. Churchill's second day at sea—when it was said in Washington that a "high British personage" might be expected to land by air at any moment. On August 6th a brief message was received from the *Potomac* to say that the President was enjoying his "cruise off New England." On the following day a cryptic message was received to the effect that "all members of the party are showing the effects of the sunning. Fishing luck is good. No destination has been announced."

By this time, however, the rumours had found public expression. At 10.45 p.m. on August 6th, Cincinnati Radio in Ohio commented in German (there are 100,000 Germans in Ohio) that "according to a report from Washington rumours show that President Roosevelt will meet Prime Minister Winston Churchill in the Atlantic. So far this news has not been denied or confirmed. It is pointed out in Washington circles that Mr. Roosevelt is already cruising in the Atlantic in the Presidential yacht, *Potomac*, and that Mr. Winston Churchill for unknown reasons is not appearing in the House these days." The Swiss radio from Berne took up this story at once, adding that it was rumoured President Roosevelt and Mr. Churchill were to meet in Canada.

On August 7th, the Washington correspondent of the *New York Herald Tribune* noted that four of the most senior officers had gone with the President "for conference with Mr. Churchill and members of a British mission." On the same day it was stated in New York that the meeting was taken for granted. The only matter for conjecture was where was it to be held? Canada, Iceland, Greenland and Newfoundland were all mentioned as possible places.

Thus a secret that could not have been kept was broadcast to the world while Mr. Churchill was in mid-Atlantic. There was consequently no point in keeping back the news of the meeting, or the text of the Atlantic Charter, until Mr. Churchill was safely at home again. It was therefore broadcast to the world by Mr. Attlee from London on Wednesday, August 14th, while the *Prince of Wales* was still at sea on her homeward voyage.

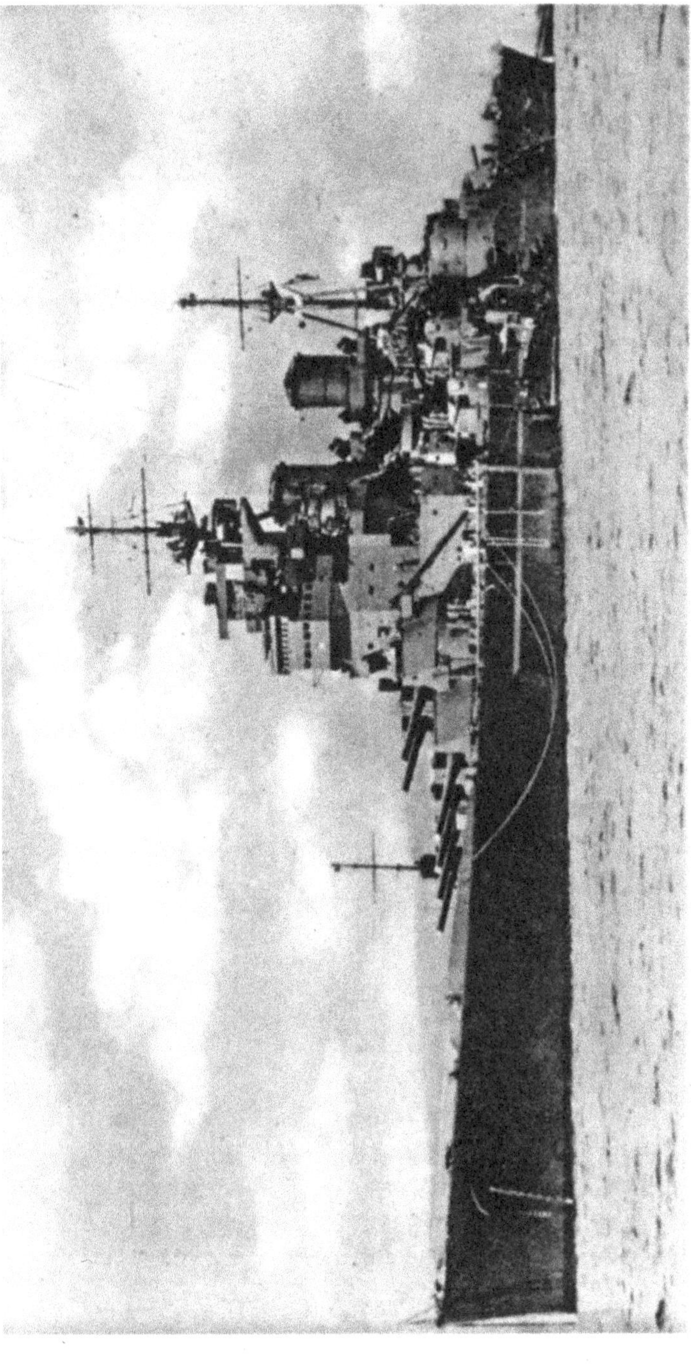

H.M.S. *Prince of Wales*

The daily meeting on board the *Prince of Wales*. (L. to R.) Admiral Sir Dudley Pound, Sir John Dill, Mr. Churchill, Sir Wilfrid Freeman

It is probable that the date of this broadcast is responsible for a remarkable error, even in official publications and Government statements, where the date of the "signing" of the Atlantic Charter is given as August 14th, two days after Mr. Churchill and Mr. Roosevelt had said good-bye. The facts are that the Atlantic Charter was never signed at all but was approved by the President and the Prime Minister while their ships were at anchor on Tuesday, August 12th, shortly before Mr. Churchill sailed on his return voyage. There exists therefore no document sealed with wax that can take its place in the State archives. The Atlantic Charter was drawn up in typescript and was redrafted time after time until it was finally agreed upon by Mr. Churchill and Mr. Roosevelt. Having agreed upon it, the text was telegraphed to London and to Washington. In London, a special meeting of the War Cabinet was called to consider it. Having agreed with all its points, the War Cabinet telegraphed its approval to Mr. Churchill while Washington telegraphed approval to the President. Thus the original Atlantic Charter is several sheets of typescript, while the Charter, as approved by the Governments of Great Britain and the United States, takes the form of two long telegrams. In the course of transmission to London four words got lost and did not appear in the British text, but they have now been inserted, as explained in the Note to Appendix A. The Atlantic Charter is clearly one of the most remarkable documents in history, and a world that has been taught by bitter experience to view documents and signatures with a certain amount of cynicism may feel that the fact that the Atlantic Charter was not signed, sealed and delivered in the usual manner may augur well for the future of Mankind.

Let us raise a standard to which
the wise and honest can repair;
the rest is in the hands of God.

GEORGE WASHINGTON, at the Constitutional
Convention at Philadelphia in 1787

I

I AM WARNED

On the morning of Saturday, the 2nd of August, 1941, I travelled to London full of curiosity, wondering why the Minister of Information should have asked me to see him without fail at eleven o'clock. It is unusual for Government departments to show exceptional activity during a Bank Holiday week-end, even in wartime, and eleven o'clock on a Saturday morning is a moment which Cabinet Ministers reserve only for the most important occasions.

The Ministry of Information is guarded by men in blue uniform who convey to the visitor, by an air of suspicion and contempt, that he is probably trying to force his way for some preposterous purpose to the intellectual giants beyond. Imagine my surprise when, instead of standing meekly with a buff form in my hand, I was taken straight up the marble stairs to the Minister's room. Such a thing had never happened to me before, and I was naturally apprehensive. Something odd was happening.

I had hardly time to study the room in which I was sitting when the door opened and a large man came hurriedly in. I had not met Brendan Bracken before, although I had seen him once or twice in the House of Commons. He had recently been appointed Minister of Information and had been in office only for ten days or so. I noticed that his hair is not red, as the newspapers insist, but a stubborn, unbrushable auburn hair so thick that it looks like a wig. Mr. Bracken is a big-boned, powerful man, and I thought him also quick, nervous and probably temperamental, but I had no inkling of the exciting state secret which at that moment he was guarding. His manner, as he rushed in and shook hands, reminded me of the news editor of an evening paper at about four o'clock during a crisis.

Men who have official dealings with the Press either refer to it frostily as "gentlemen," implying that the Press is, or ought to be, inspired by the same high motives as those which animate the speaker, or else they call it "boys," slap it on the back and attempt to establish a terrific camaraderie founded on a mutual background of clubs and pubs and craft and guile. This is a technique that can be flattering to a gentle British newspaperman because it makes him feel like a dashing American reporter in a film. Previous Ministers of Information have adopted the icy "gentlemen" method, but Brendan Bracken, I was glad to see, belongs to neither school: he is clear, concise, friendly and agreeable.

"I have an extraordinary proposition to put up to you," he began. "I want you to leave England for three weeks, but I regret to say I can't tell you where you are going or what you will see when you get there. I can only say that if you go you will see history in the making and be present at one of the great moments of the war. Will you go?"

"Yes," I replied, "of course I'll go."

"Then I can tell you this. You will leave London to-morrow, and you will leave England on Monday in a battleship. You will be at sea for about a week. You will be for several days in or near a foreign country and you will then return home in the battleship. I can tell you no more. This is what you are expected to do. You and Howard Spring, the novelist, have been chosen to describe—whatever it is you are going to see. Captain Ritchie, who writes under the name of 'Bartimæus,' is going with you, not as a writer, but as a liaison officer to help you and to keep you officially informed. I haven't yet seen Spring, who is due from Cornwall at any moment."

The thought ran through my mind while he was speaking that this mysterious affair must be a naval action, with a troop landing, perhaps in Russia. As if he had read my thoughts, Brendan Bracken said:

"It's not likely you'll hear any shooting unless Germany sends out a pocket battleship to intercept you."

"What clothes shall I pack?" I asked. "A week in a battleship can take me into the Tropics or into the Arctic circle."

"The kind you're wearing now."

So, as this was an English summer's day, it was certainly not the Tropics. Then I asked a question which seemed foolish to me at the time, because my mind was running on naval actions and troops landing on beaches. I can't imagine why I asked it, unless it was in order to gain time and perhaps learn a little more.

"Shall I pack a dinner jacket?"

"Most certainly, I should take a dinner jacket."

I knew then that, whatever the mystery, it was not a warlike but a diplomatic occasion; even so, the thought of dressing for dinner in a battleship in wartime struck me as strange.

Brendan Bracken concluded the interview:

"Be at the Admiralty to-morrow morning at eleven, and you will be given your instructions. Now good-bye and— good luck."

A gleam of what might have been almost Irish humour shone for a moment behind horn spectacles.

"How I wish I were in your shoes," he said.

I went out into Bloomsbury wondering what it was all about. It was exciting. It was like the opening of a good Buchan spy novel. Yet I reflected that it has been my unvarying experience in life, that when men wish you good luck and in the same breath long to be in your shoes, you can be sure that you are in for something certainly uncomfortable, and possibly dangerous.

Returning to my home, in Hampshire, I wrote notes cancelling my appointments for the coming three weeks, mentioning that I had been suddenly called away to Nottingham, which seemed to me to have an authentic ring about it. Among other things, I packed my Home Guard uniform, which may have been the first of its kind to cross the Atlantic. I know so well from past experience with what polite but averted eyes the Navy observes civilian clothes on spectacular occasions. I remember once, during manœuvres in the Mediterranean, being asked by a charming martinet, who is now an admiral, whether I would mind taking cover in the ward-room until the flagship had been passed because a soft hat on the quarter-deck spoilt the ship. Having packed, I spent a restless night trying to probe the immediate future: at one moment I saw myself the most envied and unpopular man in my profession; at others I saw myself drifting in mid-ocean on a raft.

While I was dressing in the morning I happened to switch on the seven o'clock news, and one item burst like a rocket into my dark speculations. President Roosevelt had left in his yacht, unaccompanied by the Press, on a fishing holiday up the New England coast! Surely there was some connection between the battleship that was so secretly departing from England on the Monday, and the sudden cruise of the President of the United States? Why should the President have decided to go fishing at that critical moment of the war? Germany was flinging herself against the Stalin Line and Japan was baring her yellow fangs in the Pacific. It was certainly an odd moment to go fishing. The more I thought of it, the more certain I became that I had found a clue to the mystery. Anyhow, the guess seemed good enough to justify the inclusion in my luggage of Baedeker's guides to *The United States* and *Canada*. Eventually *Canada*, which devotes several pages to Newfoundland, did indeed prove to be of the greatest use to me.

II

THE PRIME MINISTER'S TRAIN

On Sunday morning, August 3rd, the Admiralty was trying to look as though nothing unusual was happening. The day was warm and sunny, and London, although ragged, sand-bagged and wired, still haunted in corners by the acrid smell of recent midnight fires, looked gracious and lovely. There were more people than usual strolling up and down the Mall, but few of them noticed the line of cars drawn up outside the Admiralty, or the naval officers, carrying suit-cases and boxes, who entered them and drove away. A commander came out with a messenger who carried a geographical globe, which was placed tenderly in a taxi. So we were taking the earth with us. I wondered why.

It was a strange experience to stand for a moment out-side the Admiralty, knowing that behind the furtive activity a grey warship was waiting at some secret rendezvous; to watch the crowds passing and re-passing, unaware of the State secret which was being unfolded before their eyes on that quiet Sunday morning. Yet, I asked myself, might there not be someone in the crowd who knew—someone like that fellow on the edge of the pavement over there who was casually lighting his pipe? Would that shaggy moustache respond to a sharp pull, would that mop of greyish hair come off in the hand? Once again the vision of a raft tilted against the ocean swell came to me, and, rebuking myself for a touch of hysteria, I entered the Admiralty.

Anyone sensitive to atmosphere would readily have perceived that here the secret had touched exasperation point. Naval officers, warned individually as I had been, were emerging like conspirators from their offices, glancing swiftly along the corridors to make sure they were unobserved—to encounter their friends next door doing the same thing! They stood regarding each other's suit-cases with comic bewilderment, "Good lord, Freddie, are you coming, too?" And they departed together like men on whom conspiracy has died.

As I was taken to the office of the Press Division, I reflected that State secrecy is a cynical procedure. Warned by centuries of experience, the State is aware that because man's nature is frail and his vanity colossal anything known to more than one person cannot be termed a secret. Therefore it splits up its secret into many fragments, like a jig-saw puzzle, and gives to each man his share, trusting that sufficient fragments will not be pieced together to form a recognisable pattern. It is only at the top that a few men, as few as possible, know the whole picture.

Entering the Director's office, I saw that Howard Spring had already arrived. He is a gentle, slender man with a lot of iron-grey hair. From a narrow face gaze, two extremely live eyes which can be either exceedingly melancholy or extremely humorous, and are always shrewd and observant. Lord Beaverbrook brought him from Manchester to London in 1931, where he made a reputation as a book reviewer and then performed the extraordinary feat, for a book reviewer, of writing several best-selling novels; which, of course, is what all reviewers would like to do. Departing from news-papers on a flood-tide of royalties, he now lives with a yacht on an estuary in Cornwall, and is, despite his eyes, a truly happy and contented man.

"Can you tell me what this is all about?" he asked.

"I was hoping you might be able to tell me," I replied.

"I know absolutely nothing," he continued. "I came up from Cornwall yesterday to see Brendan Bracken, fully expecting to catch a late train home. And here I am. I have no clothes except these I'm wearing and I have no teeth. All my teeth were taken out last week and I haven't yet got my new set. So here I am, clotheless and toothless, going, God knows where . . ."

The Director of the Press Division entered, maddeningly hearty and uncommunicative.

"Even if I knew where you are going," he said, "I shouldn't be allowed to tell you. But I really don't know. All I can do is to give you these instructions. Be on Number Four Platform, Marylebone Station before twelve-thirty. Your names are on the list and you are expected. Well, good-bye and—good luck."

As unconscious of our fate as two rabbits in transit, we drove through those peaceful Sunday streets to the only main-line station in London which is not entirely hideous. Spring was inclined to resign himself to destiny with a care-less shrug. It was like travelling in a taxi with Hamlet. Only when I told him of Roosevelt's fishing trip did his eyes change from tragedy to acute attention.

"Do you think that America is coming into the war?" I asked. "Is it possible that we are going to see the American Fleet steam out to battle stations?"

"I wonder," said Spring. "By the way, I believe you've sailed in battleships before. Can you remember if the food is unusually tough?"

So we came to Marylebone Station. It was a perfect study in the casual. No one could have guessed that one of the greatest secrets of the war was due to leave in less than half an hour. A few suburban trains were arriving and departing; a few passengers were strolling about; the newspaper stalls were shut, but trestle tables erected near them offered the Sunday papers. And when we looked at Platform Four, thinking that at last something would be revealed to us, we saw naval and military officers walking casually past the barrier as if they were going to Rickmansworth. Knowing what we knew, it was most impressive. Edgar Wallace could not have done it better.

The ticket collector, who was probably a detective in disguise, asked our names and checked them on a list, and we passed on to the platform, where a long train was drawn up. As I walked towards it, a sleeping-car attendant wearing a snuff-brown livery greeted me by name, which surprised me until I realised that he must have read the labels on my luggage.

"Good morning, Mr. Morton; I hope you're well, sir," he said, like a family retainer welcoming the squire home. I followed him into the car, thinking how odd life is, for those who travel without railway tickets experience either gaol or a regal reception.

"And where are we going?" I asked the friendly attendant. The smile died on his face.

"Sorry, sir," he said. "I'm not at liberty to say."

But the sleeping-cars had told me this: that we were not

going to Dover, Harwich, Portsmouth, Fishguard, or indeed to any port in England or Wales, but to the north of Scotland, for that is the only journey in Great Britain, if you leave London soon after noon, which justifies a sleeper.

The clock was now almost at the half hour. I had walked the length of the train in the hope of seeing the personage, or personages, for whom so grand a train had been ordered. There was no sign of him or of them. The dining-car tables were set for luncheon. There were vases of sweet peas and cornflowers on them. There was a regal little saloon, but no one inside it. It was uncanny. Our fellow travellers were a few staff officers, one brigadier, a colonel or two, some majors and a few naval captains and commanders. As the clock struck the half-hour I leaned from the carriage window expecting to see the platform gates swing wide to admit a royal Daimler, or perhaps even Winston Churchill— yes, that fantastic thought did indeed flash through my mind! But no, nothing happened. A whistle blew, slowly the train moved from the platform; and a number of Scotland Yard detectives, whom I had not noticed before, relaxed and felt for their pipes.

I lunched at a table with a colonel, who introduced himself as Colonel Hollis. I was to learn later that he was the Senior Assistant Secretary in the office of the Minister of Defence. We admired the scenery as the train ran out of the Middlesex lowlands into the Chiltern Hills, from whose gentle heights we saw the beauty of Buckinghamshire lying about us: hill, valley and beechwood. I knew that Colonel Hollis must know the secret, and, in order not to embarrass him and to make my own position clear, I told him that I knew nothing except that we were obviously going to

Scotland. He smiled and glanced out of the window, but I felt that he would like to have been able to enlighten me. And the train rushed on.

After lunch I returned to my sleeper, intending to read a book, but while I was unpacking a bag I noticed that the train was slowing down to a stop. My window faced the up-rails of a small Country station on which I saw an excited crowd of people laughing, waving and pointing to someone on the other side. I went out into the corridor to see the reason for their excitement and, looking through a window, I was richly rewarded.

Winston Churchill was standing on the platform wearing a blue suit, a yachting cap and smoking a cigar. The smile with which he had answered the greetings from the opposite platform had not yet gone from his face. Beside him stood a man I knew, General Sir John Dill, Chief of the Imperial General Staff, and another whom I knew by sight, Admiral Sir Dudley Pound, the First Sea Lord. There were also an Air-Chief Marshal, who turned out to be Sir Wilfrid Freeman, Vice-Chief of the Air Staff, Sir Alexander Cadogan, of the Foreign Office, and a tall, unsmiling man who was until recently Professor Lindemann, and is now Lord Cherwell, friend and confidant of the Prime Minister.

As I watched them board the train two coaches away from me I heard someone calling my name. I went towards him and met Brendan Bracken, hatless, his auburn hair ruffled, his face beaming with delight.

"Well, you see who's on the train?" he asked eagerly. The train began to move. "Good luck!" he said as he leaped down on the platform.

I thought his action a kind and friendly one, and I was grateful to him. It showed understanding, too, for, although I had not mentioned it, he knew that, having swallowed his secret whole, hook, line and sinker, as I had done, I had disrupted my private life in order to take part in it. And perhaps he was anxious to tell me that virtue had been rewarded, which, as I say, was a friendly thought and shows a good heart.

I sat talking with Spring in our day coach all afternoon as the train rushed north. We could hardly believe even then that the Prime Minister and the Chiefs of Staff would cross the Atlantic in a battleship. Surely they would have flown in a bomber? On the other hand, what other destination, and what other appointment except one with the President of the United States, could have drawn such a galaxy from England in wartime? There could also be little doubt that it would be true to Churchill's character and temperament to refuse to fly the Atlantic, but to dare U-boat and bomber and entrust himself to the British Navy. If so, it was, we agreed, the best of all the Churchill stories, better than Omdurman, South Africa, Sidney Street, Antwerp or the trenches at Ploegsteert.

Colonel Hollis came into the carriage and lit a cigarette.

"I've been talking to the Prime Minister's secretary," he said, "and he agrees with me that it's nonsense for you both to remain in the dark any longer. We're going to Newfoundland to meet the President of the United States. We are to cross the Atlantic in the *Prince of Wales*. While the President and the Prime Minister confer together, the three Chiefs of Staff will meet their opposite numbers on the American side. So now you can sleep in peace. . . ."

"How close a secret is it?" we asked.

"The best-kept secret I can remember in Whitehall," he replied. "It has been put about that the Prime Minister is going north to inspect an operation, which is quite a normal proceeding. Only one or two men in London know that he is really leaving England. Such care was taken that nothing should leak out that several officers now on the train, who work together in the same rooms in the Admiralty and the War Office, did not know that their companions were coming until they met at Marylebone Station this morning."

"And how is the Prime Minister?"

"Well, you'll see," replied the Colonel. "He's rather like a boy who's been let out of school suddenly. He says it's the only holiday he's had since the war."

We dined in high spirits that evening, sensing that we were bound on a good adventure. Whether we were conscious that we were moving on the stream of history, I don't know. I suppose that realisation comes later. No one, I think, was more cheerful or more conscious of the adventure, and maybe of the history, too, than the chief traveller. We could hear his resonant House of Commons voice raised cheerfully from time to time in the next coach. He admired the golden harvest fields as we flew north.

I saw him sitting in the parlour car, and I thought that we should have brought a painter with us. It was an admirable picture. Mr. Churchill had changed into a peculiar garment well known in Whitehall and Downing Street called "the P.M.'s siren suit" or, less reverently, "the Teddy Bear." It is a garment of battle-dress design, made of wool almost Air Force blue in colour and fitted with a zip-fastener from neck to waist. It can be put on in a second and discarded as rapidly. Mr. Churchill wears this siren suit during his nocturnal hours of working, during air raids and when he summons a War Cabinet in the middle of the night. It is a garment which has absorbed a great deal of its wearer's personality, and is already acquiring a definitely historical appearance. Should it outlast the War, or should someone with a sufficiently high sense of his duty to posterity preserve it when it is worn out, then the suit is clearly destined for a glass case in years to come.

With this garment making him seem rounder, plumper and more of a character than ever, Mr. Churchill sat with a shaded reading-light at his elbow. He had ceased to draw on a cigar which had gone out. He wore a pair of reading glasses. On chairs round about him were despatch cases and boxes which gushed a river of papers and documents. While he picked up one of them, read it, discarded it or made a note in the margin, he was dictating to two secretaries who sat near with note-books on their knees. In the background was a gleam of gold lace on the cuffs of the First Sea Lord and a glow of red tabs and war ribbons on the tunic of the Chief of the Imperial General Staff. All the time the little room with its shaded lights vibrated with movement, and beyond the windows the tall stacks and roof lines of some Midland town swung round towards us, grew larger and flashed past.

At Leicester we stopped for a new engine. It was not yet black-out time, and the windows were uncurtained. A shunting engine was stationary on rails opposite the Prime Minister's saloon. The driver of this engine was an old man with grey hair who wore a cap flattened by age and grease and oil, and he was leaning from his cab to exchange some pleasantry with a friend on the line. Happening to lift his head, he became aware that he was separated by not more than six yards from an apparition that bore every resemblance to Winston Churchill. Although the brains of engine drivers move with considerable rapidity, it took him a second or two to become convinced that the vision was a reality, during which time his mouth opened and a startled smile, which changed to one of great pleasure, crossed his blackened face. Lifting the oily cap from his head, he leaned out and shouted, "Good old Winston!" And the Prime Minister, lifting his cigar an inch or so from his mouth, gave one of his most roguish smiles. Then the train moved on.

"Leicester!" commented Mr. Churchill. "I once fought an election there, but they didn't want me."

When darkness had fallen, we saw the Rock of Edinburgh lying against the stars. No lights climbed the acropolis, as they used to do, and we ran into a station that was as silent and ghostly as a tomb. The platform was closed to the public. Policemen stood everywhere watching. Here we exchanged a stained and heated engine for a fresh green Pacific that drew us out again into the night.

Soon after this I went to bed and attempted to read. But all the time my mind returned to this extraordinary adventure and to my home. I wondered whether the alert had yet sounded, whether the intermittent Diesels were crossing the night sky like old steamboats, whether bombs were rattling the nursery door; and, mixed with anxiety for those whom I had left to face alone the perils of a night in war-time England, came a thrilling sense of freedom and escape. I realised for the first time what a siege this War is for England.

President Roosevelt leaning on the arm of his son, Capt. Elliott Roosevelt, greets Mr. Churchill in the *Augusta* and is handed a letter from the King

Mr. Churchill watching the President's destroyer depart on Sunday, August 10th, 1941

I was like a member of some beleaguered garrison sent out on a mission under cover of darkness, who finds himself rejoicing in freedom of movement as his feet touch the grass and as his eyes see the outline of hills he used to know before the gates were shut.

It was a sharp exultant gladness, not untouched by a feeling of guilt; for I had performed no garrison duties that night. I had not inspected the black-out; I had not removed the distributor arm; I had not seen the stirrup pumps and sand buckets placed in position; I had held no converse with Warden or Home Guard. In other words, I was outside the fortress for the first time for nearly two years! If in movement and change, in the sudden falling away of duties that had become a habit, I could experience such an uplifting sense of escape, what of the man in the coach ahead, who, since Norway, had carried upon his shoulders the burden of England's fight for existence? It would be interesting to study him in the course of the next three weeks, were I given the opportunity. I had seen Winston Churchill many a time during the past twenty years—in the House of Commons, at state ceremonies, at Guildhall banquets, at all manner of public functions, and last year, as a November wind was blowing through the windows of Westminster Abbey, I might have touched his sleeve as he stood with bowed head, his face unreadable, watching the ashes of Neville Chamberlain, the man of peace, interred in wartime London. Yet I had never spoken to him.

III

H.M.S. "*PRINCE OF WALES*"

I AWAKENED soon after six o'clock. We were pounding
through a cold country where mists decapitated the hills and
steamed down into clefts and corries. Crofts stood in lonely
places, sheep dotted the rocky landscape. Now and again the
wheels machine-gunned across a girder bridge, and I saw a
brown river foaming through a ravine below. I knew we
must be far off to the North. Snow shields made of old railway sleepers were erected near the line at places where drifts
accumulate in the winter. But, owing to the caution of the
Scot, wayside railway stations bore not the reduced type
common in England, but no names at all. So it was impossible to say exactly where we were.

The friendly attendant in the brown uniform brought
me a cup of tea and two biscuits.

"And where are we now?" I asked.

His morning greeting expired on his lips.

"Sorry, sir, I'm not allowed to tell you."

But the secret was wearing thin, for even the least observant traveller, must have gathered that we were well to the
north of Caithness. Sometimes I caught a glimpse to the
right of a steely sea falling on a desolate coast.

Soon after breakfast we arrived at a station which

without much difficulty I recognised as Thurso. The usual
Scots mist was turning to determined rain. A line of damp
W.R.N.S. stood in the open, contemplating our stained
sleeping-cars with pleasant anticipation, the mist sparkling
in their hair; a few inhabitants were grouped about the station entrance; sailors in oilskins waited for the luggage, and
under an ash tree outside the local Rolls Royce stood ready
for the distinguished visitor.

I did not see the Prime Minister step from his coach and
inspect, as I suppose he did, the damp young women, but,
together with Spring and members of the party, I entered a
military car which took us to a high sea wall at Scrabster. We
saw a drifter with the lovely name of *Smiling Morn* rising
and falling to the harbour swell. As soon as we were aboard
she turned and made for a destroyer which was anchored in
the bay; and we stood watching the dour grey cluster of
houses with the mist low over them and the rain falling,
thinking it was a melancholy last glimpse of home.

The destroyer was called the *Oribi*, which is the name of a
South African antelope. The young men who control her
destiny welcomed us aboard with considerable reverence,
and led us down steep steel ladders into the ward-room. She
was a new ship and they were tremendously house-proud;
indeed, they reminded me of young wives in their first home
who expect visitors to go into a bathroom in ecstasy and see
a frigidaire for the first time in their lives. It was only by exer-
cising firm determination combined with tact that I excused
myself from being taken to admire the engines. As we sat in
the pleasant little ward-room, a cat with her newly-born
family in a box by the electric fire adding to the domesticity
of the scene, our hosts asked us in a whisper if it were really

true that Winston was the distinguished personage who was going to sea in the *Prince of Wales*. We said yes, and they said that he was an absolute wizard and a game old cock. They asked where we were going—Russia, America?—and we replied that it was a close secret. They apologised for asking, but wondered whether we were going to see President Roosevelt, which would be a jolly good show, and just the sort of thing old Winston would do.

We were surprised to hear that even the Navy was guessing, and we asked what the *Prince of Wales* thought about it. The young men told us that the officers of the *Prince of Wales* had held a sweepstake on the identity of their visitor and the nature of his mission. Some of the officers had drawn rather outside chances, such as "Taking Hess back to Germany," "Taking Mr. Cochran's Young Ladies to Dakar," and one officer, regarded as an also ran, had drawn the guess, "Taking Winston Churchill to see Roosevelt."

Our conversation was interrupted by the sound of feet on steel plates overhead. We went on deck in time to see Mr. Churchill and the Chiefs of Staff step aboard from a drifter. The mist had now settled into a firm drizzle, and the Prime Minister was offered shelter.

"No," he said; "the bridge."

The *Oribi* throbbed, her anchors came up and, like her nimble namesake, she flung herself across the waters of the bay, meeting outside the strength of the cross-seas that sent her nose up into the air and down again to a whip of spray. I went up on the bridge and saw Mr. Churchill there loyally attached to his cigar, his collar up, his eyes screwed against the wind and the driving rain. Beside him, admirably at home, stood the First Sea Lord, and Sir John Dill, who had let down the chin-strap of his service cap and faced the wind with greater confidence.

The young men of the *Oribi* were determined to show the Prime Minister what that superlative destroyer could do, and we fairly raced across that frightful turmoil of water in whose channel, only six to eight miles wide, the Atlantic Ocean and the North Sea meet. Clouds hung above Orkney and the grey mist was like a veil over the hills, and soon we were steaming between Hoy and South Ronaldshay into the less turbulent waters of Scapa Flow.

We saw, a giant among giants, the splendid ship that was to be our home, her great guns pointing fore and aft, her crew drawn up on deck. How beautiful she looked that morning as she appeared out of the mist, full of power, strength and pride. As we approached her, bells rang in our engine-room, we slowed and, tilting slightly against the sea, swung round to her and, as we did so, we saw that the battleship, which from a distance had looked so graceful and so lithe, now towered above us like a mighty hill of steel. Far above us the fifteen hundred odd members of her crew stood mustered on the decks, the bosuns stood at the gangway, the Officer of the Watch with his telescope, the Captain, the Royal Marines with their band upon the quarterdeck; and it was interesting to watch the expression of the *Prince of Wales* as we came alongside, for every pair of eyes was upon the bridge of the *Oribi,* where a man was smoking a cigar; and you see lips forming words and almost hear a whisper go right round the battleship—"*It's Winston!*"

He crossed the gangway from ship to ship, and as his foot touched the quarter-deck he saluted and then shook hands with Captain Leach—a tall, elegant figure with a telescope tucked beneath his arm. Gradually the ship's company melted away to its duties, there was a sound of brassy cheerful music as the Marines moved off and soon the ship was ready for sea.

Standing in the shadow of a gun turret, holding a soft felt hat on his head, a loose American overcoat of brown tweed blowing about him, was a thin man of extraordinary pallor and fragility. He looked as I have seen men look when they come out of a nursing home, yet this man had just flown from Moscow in a bomber. His name was Harry Hopkins, President Roosevelt's friend and the administrator of the Lease-Lend Act. He approached Mr. Churchill, who, at the sight of him, cried happily:

"Ah, my dear friend, how are you? And how did you find Stalin?"

They shook hands and linked arms.

"I must tell you all about it," said Harry Hopkins in a slow, wonderfully weary American voice.

Together, with arms still linked, they moved towards a hatchway and went below.

A bugle sounded. A bell rang. There was an almost imperceptible tremble in the deck underfoot and, looking towards the shore, I saw the hills moving and I said, "We're off!"

A young naval officer came up and saluted. His name was Lieutenant Dyer-Smith. He had been detailed to show me to my cabin. We went below into the electrically-lit depths of the ship, his nimble feet running easily down almost perpendicular ladders, mine following slowly and cautiously. We came to a place where Marine sentries stood on duty at a desk. Rows of revolvers were chained to the wall in a glass case. A flight of steps led to a lower deck in whose narrow steel alleys midshipmen slung their hammocks by night and stowed them by day as if they were in the *Victory*. Along a side of an alley was a row of officers' cabins, and above the door of one—No. 27—I read my name printed on a card.

"I hope you'll be comfortable," said the young man.

As battleship cabins go, it was almost luxurious. The bunk was built into the white curve of the ship's side, and there was a writing desk with side drawers and a lot of cupboards. There was a wash basin with hot and cold water, and there were plenty of electric lights. But the place shook like an aspen, and there was a steady roar of thunder.

"It's a bit noisy, isn't it?" I remarked.

"It's over the propellor shaft," said Dyer-Smith, "but I expect you'll get used to it."

It was an optimistic thought. I knew that I should never get used to it. I was appalled by the thought of living there, and trying to sleep there, for the next three weeks. The revolving shaft thundered below like a battery of Goss presses at the peak of a run. The vibration was almost worse than the noise. Small objects were given a life of their own. A penny, a bunch of keys, a book, a pencil, all dancing out of time, slowly jumped towards the precipice of the locker's edge and one by one fell upon the cabin floor.

"We're doing a good thirty knots," said the young man. "It's not always as bad as this," he added, apologetically.

"Whose cabin is it?" I asked.

"Mine," he replied.

I apologised for turning him out, for I know so well the heart-burning that goes on in a battleship when distinguished personages and their suites and attendants render half the ship homeless. There are few things a naval officer hates more than an invasion of the only little bit of privacy left to him; the only place where he may express individuality in a pair of brilliant pyjamas or a silk dressing-gown; the only place where the softer emotions may be visibly expressed in an expensively framed photograph of a woman or a child; where such objects as a fishing-rod, a gun, or a bag of golf clubs bring into a life at sea some memory of the land.

He brushed my apology aside with a smile, and his official manner dropped.

"It's a great privilege for the ship to be taking the Prime Minister to sea, sir," he said eagerly. "We're all tremendously proud of it, and I'm pleased that you've got my cabin."

He then became official again and, approaching the bunk, indicated a slight swelling on the floor.

"That's where a *Bismarck* shell came in," he said. "It didn't do much damage, but it's left a bump, as you can see."

"You were in the action?"

"Rather! We got in some good shooting, but we were called off just as things were getting exciting. We were very fed up at the time."

A Royal Marine, coatless and with braces over a khaki shirt, came in and began to unpack my luggage.

"This is your servant, Creese," said Dyer-Smith.

Creese nodded and withdrew my Home Guard uniform with an expression of gloom.

"Better send the trousers to the ship's tailor, sir," he said. "He'll get all this mud off and put a knife crease into them."

It was a grand idea. They came back that night with all the Hampshire Upper Greensand removed, and a crease in them that was a joy to behold.

And where was Mr. Churchill? I found that Captain Leach had given up his quarters to the Prime Minister, and had gone to his sea cabin on the bridge. The Captain's quarters, or rather the Admiral's quarters, for the *Prince of Wales* was fitted up as a flagship, comprised—as house agents put it—a spacious drawing-room furnished with chintz-covered settees and arm-chairs, a dining-room, a bedroom, a bathroom, and a pantry, all situated in the stern of the ship. Other cabins had been vacated by senior officers for the First Sea Lord, Sir John Dill, Sir Wilfrid Freeman, Lord Cherwell, Sir Alexander Cadogan, Commander C. R. Thompson, the Prime Minister's Personal Assistant, and Mr. J. M. Martin, Private Secretary. They were to take their meals with the Prime Minister in the Captain's quarters.

The remainder of the party were: Brigadier V. Dykes, Director of Plans, War Office; Colonel L. C. Hollis and Colonel E. I. C. Jacob, of the office of the Minister of Defence; Captain B. B. Schofield, R.N., Director of the Trade Division of the Admiralty; Commander M. G. Goodenough, R.N., Plans Division, Admiralty; Paymaster-Captain Brockman, R.N., Secretary to the First Sea Lord; Captain Nutting, Military Assistant to the C.I.G.S.; Group-Captain W. M. Yool, Staff officer to the Vice-Chief of the Air Staff; Captain R. P. Pim, R.N.V.R., and Lt.-Commander H. W. McMullen, R.N.V.R., both of the Operations Room,

the Admiralty, and, finally, Captain Ritchie, Spring and
myself. The thirteen of us were made temporary members
of the ward-room. We occupied the cabins of officers who
had been turned out for us, and we ate in the ward-room
with our hosts.

When I went on deck again, the *Prince of Wales* was
steaming towards the open sea. Three destroyers escorted
us—*Harvester, Havelock* and *Hesperus*—one ahead and two
abeam, rising and falling on the grey swell. From the quarter-deck I looked back and saw Orkney fade in mist, and
the thought, which I tried to banish from my mind, of
another mission came to me—the only one in recent history to be compared with this: when Kitchener left for
Russia during the last war in H.M.S. *Hampshire*, and met
death off the coast of Hoy. It was not a pleasant thought and
I wondered if that tragic voyage had flashed through any
brain in Whitehall when the Prime Minister expressed his
intention to cross the Atlantic. What a target we were—
Winston Churchill and the Chiefs of Staff! We were
undoubtedly the best target that Hitler had been offered.
Could he sink us, could he send the loathed and detested
Churchill to the bottom of the sea—the monster who alone
among English statesmen had seen through him and had the
courage to say so in days of our colossal inertia—what a
shattering blow to the confidence of all nations still fighting
to be free! How many U-boats were we worth, I wondered;
how many long-range bombers? That he would try to attack
us, I had no doubt at all. I wondered at what point in our
voyage it was likely to come, and whether from under the
sea or from the air. I cannot pretend to have enjoyed these
reflections and, having a horror of drowning, I noted with

dismay that no life-boats were to be seen; instead, a number of rafts known as Carley floats suggested most vividly the speed with which, a modern ship can sink.

Spring came up, and as we were talking we were interrupted by a well-known voice; turning, we found ourselves looking into the twinkling blue eyes of Winston Churchill.

"Introduce me to these gentlemen," he said to his Private Secretary. Martin did so, and we shook hands. Colonel Hollis had been right. Winston had been let out of school. He was enjoying himself enormously, loving every minute of it. His cigar was well alight, and he watched us with a humorous twinkle in his eye from under the peak of his yachting cap.

"I hope we shall have an interesting and enjoyable voyage," he said. Then, with the slight hesitation and change of voice which are so effective on the radio, he added dryly, as if as an after-thought, "And one not entirely without profit."

He stood there looking mischievous, broad-shouldered and aggressive, then, with a friendly wave of his hand, turned to walk the quarter-deck.

IV

"PIMPERNEL SMITH"

THE ward-room of the *Prince of Wales* was a large room some sixty feet in length and its width was the width of the ship. You stepped straight into it from the quarterdeck. It was divided into two parts: on the port side was the ante-room, furnished with easy chairs, a club lounge, a bookcase containing *Chambers' Encyclopedia* and a number of novels and other works which reflected the innocent literary taste of the mess; and on the starboard side was the dining room. In the dining-room were two long tables and a hatch where Royal Marines in white mess jackets served the food. Above the mantelpiece hung an irreverent Gilray caricature of the Prince Regent, presented in a moment of characteristic generosity by Lieut.-Commander George Ferguson.

At the end of the ante-room was a small bar, which was opened before lunch and dinner, where gin was sold at 3d. and whiskey at 5d. a glass. But that, although impressive, was not the most impressive thing about it. Above the bar a piece of white steel had curled round and hung from the roof like a wood shaving. It was a relic of the *Bismarck* action. When the ship had been repaired after the action it was decided to leave that one memento.

It was sheer delight to find myself after many years in
the atmosphere of a ward-room, which is that of a grown-up
public school. I can enjoy this atmosphere indefinitely so
long as I can go ashore now and then to stretch my legs and
buy a book or a newspaper; but to be at sea in a ward-room
is after a week or so a restless experience. By that time the
illustrations in the magazines are maddeningly familiar,
the newspapers are limp with reading and you find yourself
reading, with acute nausea, the advertisements for rope in
the *Yachting Times*.

It is also delightful to enter the society of a battleship, a
society that never varies. You have the Captain, known as
"the Skipper" or "the Old Man"; the Commander, known
as "the Bloke"; the Paymaster-Commander, known always
as "Pay," the Schoolmaster, "Schoolie"; the Torpedo Officer,
"Torps," and Gunnery Officer, "Guns"; the Chaplain, "the
Padre"and the Dentist, "Toothie." It is an instructive hierar-
chy, on the surface uniform, but below the surface, full of
surprising individuality. In big ships, and especially modern
battleships like the *Prince of Wales*, it sometimes happens that
so many specialists are gathered together from the edges
and corners of the Fleet that the ward-room becomes
slightly stand-offish, almost donnish. But I was glad to discover that the *Prince of Wales,* although a battleship, was as
friendly as a destroyer. So proud were the officers to be
taking Winston Churchill to sea—and so delighted that the
"P.O.W." and not the "K.G.5," as they called their sister ship,
had been chosen for the mission—that they had, for the
first time in my experience, given up their cabins with
pleasure. We shone In a glory reflected upon us from
Downing Street.

Among the many good fellows it is a little difficult to single out two, but I do so because I met Quinn and Ferguson within the first half hour and enjoyed their friendship from that moment. Surgeon-Commander Quinn was a handsome, courtly Irishman full of wit and humour, a man proud of his ship and of his place in it, and he was admired not only by his fellow officers but by the whole ship's company. Lieut-Commander Ferguson, R.N.V.R., reminded me of a young Cyril Maude. He was probably forty but he looked no more than twenty-five. He might have appeared as he was, and at any moment, upon any stage, but preferably a musical comedy stage, and have played the part of a typical British naval officer. He was almost too good to be true. He had a pink face and a pair of pale blue eyes; and I never knew him to descend from the high eyrie on which he spent his hours of duty without some amusing happening to relate or some preposterous story he had just remembered. Life was full of rich flavours for George Ferguson, and his vitality was remarkable. As he entered the ward-room, or rather as he, quite unconsciously, made an entrance, spinning his cap on a peg or a table, he brought with him an improbable air of fox-hunting. I expected him to cry "Yoicks" or "Gone away!" and I was not surprised to hear that he had a close connection with a pack of hounds in the New Forest. Quinn told me that Ferguson had been badly smashed up in an air raid on Portsmouth. He had a fractured spine, a fractured pelvis and a collapsed lung, and no one thought it possible that he could recover. But in a remarkably short time he emerged from hospital, as bright as a pint of quicksilver, and rejoined his ship.

I was standing with Quinn and Ferguson in the ante-room just before dinner on the first night at sea, when a hush spread through the room and a preliminary crackle sounded in a loud speaker.

"The Skipper's going to broadcast," someone said.

Loud speakers stationed in all parts of the ship are linked with a microphone on the bridge, and I was told that during the *Bismarck* action Captain Leach kept the whole ship's company informed by wireless of every move in the battle.

We now heard his voice telling us that we had on board the Prime Minister and the Chiefs of Staff, who were going to Placentia Bay, Newfoundland, to meet the President of the United States. "We expect to arrive there on the fore-noon of Saturday," he concluded. It was then Monday. We had four and a half days of the Atlantic before us.

There is no formality in a battleship in war-time. The ship may go into action at any moment and a proportion of the officers are always at action stations. Dressing for dinner is, of course, a thing of the past, but those officers not on watch or otherwise employed, put on winged collars with black bow ties, a slight concession to the vanished formalities. Dinner was served, as in peace-time, by Royal Marine mess servants in white jackets. Now and again a young officer would come blinking into the ante-room like a breath of the storm wear-ing a thick duffel coat and swathed about with blue scarves; flinging off those garments on the pegs outside, he would sit down to dinner without further ceremony.

I told the Roman Catholic chaplain, who was sitting next to me at dinner, that I was surprised to discover in war-time so little difference in the general structure of a ship's life. I had expected to find everything changed.

"There is an old saying in the Navy," said the Padre, "that the difference between war and peace is that in war the target hits back."

I had noticed that all the sailors were wearing lifebelts, known as Mae Wests, but, so far as I could see, the officers were not doing so. The Padre lifted the edge of his waistcoat, and I saw that the man of God was taking no risks. I wondered whether I had been rash to leave my life-belt so far away in my cabin, especially as I had been handed a type-written paper telling me where to go and what to do should the ship go into action. "You will find a life-belt in your cabin which should always be worn at sea," said this notice.

After dinner we learned from a member of the Downing Street entourage that "the P.M."—or "the Prime" as some call him—had brought with him a number of films and that it was his intention to hold a film show after dinner, to which we were all invited.

No sooner was dinner over and the tables cleared, than the Marines began to move chairs and couches from the ante-room into the dining-room to form the front row. The dining-room chairs were produced for the officers, the ship's cinema operator erected a screen and put up his projector; and so the scene was set. We took our places in "the sixpennies," as we inevitably called them, leaving the arm-chairs in the front row for the exalted ones.

The door at the end of the ward-room opened. Sir John Dill came in wearing a dinner jacket. Sir Wilfrid Freeman and Sir Alexander Cadogan and Lord Cherwell were also in dinner jackets. The First Sea Lord had remained in uniform. Then came Mr. Harry Hopkins in a dinner jacket, and, last of all, Winston Churchill beaming all over and emanating a terrific good nature, wearing the mess dress of the Royal Yacht Squadron. This is a navy-blue mess jacket with brass buttons on coat and cuffs, a boiled shirt and blue trousers. We rose to our feet. Mr. Churchill beamed a benediction upon us for a moment, then bowed, motioned us to be seated. The lights went out, and the film was *Pimpernel Smith*.

It was a film with moments, some good and some improbable, which concerns the rescue of victims from Nazi Germany by a modern English prototype of the Scarlet Pimpernel. There were several reels, and whenever one came to an end there was a whirring noise from the projector and the lights went up. Mr. Churchill at these moments turned to those nearest him and said "Jolly good," or "What do you think about it?"; and settled down with his cigar to await the next reel. You might have thought that he had not one care in the world. He possesses the ability to shut his mind at will either to worry or work and to live entirely in the present. He can come from a War Cabinet having made a great decision and enjoy an hour of Laurel and Hardy, carrying the weight of the War as if it were a bag of feathers. Then, the film over, his mind ceases to coast and, slipping into gear again, he gets down to work. It is said that on August 4th, 1914, when Downing Street was in a condition of great emotion, Winston was discovered deep in a club chair with a novel. A horrified friend, who did not know that the First Lord had mobilised the British Navy on his own responsibility and that the Fleet was already at battle stations, approached him and said:—

"How can you sit there reading a novel on this of all nights?"

Mr. Churchill among a group of American sailors

The Prime Minister and the Chiefs of Staff with men of the *Prince of Wales*

Winston looked up and knocked off an inch of cigar ash. "Well, I've done everything that can be done," he said. "What do you expect me to do?" And he went on reading.

As the film proceeded, I found my attention straying from screen to audience. We were an infinitely more exciting drama. The blacked-out warship closed for action, escorted by three spectral destroyers, was forging ahead at full speed through seas where U-boats lay in wait, not dreaming that the supreme prize of a pirate's life lay upon those waters. The battleship was ready for action. The guns were manned. From bridge to crow's-nest experienced eyes swept the ocean with night glasses. The whole ship knew that at any moment it might have to fight. Yet in the wardroom of that ship, a large room that rose and fell to the sea, vibrating slightly to the mighty turbines, sat the Prime Minister of Great Britain with the Chiefs of Staff, enjoying a film as if they were on a holiday cruise. They had bathed and changed into dinner clothes as if they were at home in England in peace-time. Never I think would Hitler have hated Churchill more than at that moment, could he have seen him, seated deep in an arm-chair in the *Prince of Wales*, white shirt-front bulging, an indulgent smile upon his face, a cigar in his mouth, and, outside—the perilous battleground of the North Atlantic.

It was a sight I shall never forget. It would have appealed enormously to André Maurois, and other friendly foreigners who have noted with appreciation, not unmixed with amusement, that the English have a genius for transforming the extraordinary into the common-place. And here perhaps was a supreme instance of that refusal to be dramatic, which nevertheless has the effect of true drama. Suppose the roles

had been changed. Suppose Hitler had been crossing a
North Atlantic haunted by British submarines in company
with Goering, Goebbels and Ribbentrop; can we imagine
in the interior of their ship a scene quite like that in the
Prince of Wales? I think not.

During a change of reel, Mr. Churchill half turned in
his chair to reveal a pink and happy face to the officers
seated behind him. In a ringing voice, he asked a young
Lieutenant what he thought of the film, then, turning
away abruptly, he put the same question to the First Sea
Lord, thus switching from one end of the Royal Navy to
the other. I found myself indulging in reflections on that
old subject of personal magnetism. It was interesting to
see how Winston Churchill, without appearing to have
made any bid for it, had gained the complete attention of
the officers. No matter how brief, or conversational or
unimportant might be any remark made by him, it would
be eagerly caught and repeated in a whisper. Not only
was there a natural interest in this close-up of a famous
man in a moment of relaxation, but there was also an
immediate and affectionate response to the overwhelm-
ing atmosphere of good nature and well being which
Winston Churchill can radiate in his moments of ease.
Bleak and cutting as he can be in anger, biting as he can
be in his contempt, and sharp as he can be in criticism, he
can, in moments of geniality, borrow the merriment of
Falstaff and something of Mr. Pickwick's determination
that everyone shall have a good time, whether he wants
to or not. I watched him closely when he made a joke as
the lights went up and I observed him by the light from the
screen; and I thought:

"This man is many men, and mixed up in him is Falstaff, Mr. Pickwick and Hamlet. What a mixture, yet what an English mixture!"

The film over, Mr. Churchill rose, pulled down the Royal Yacht Squadron waistcoat, bowed, bestowed upon us a parting benevolence and disappeared. And we saw, with a start of surprise, that it was midnight.

V

WE LOSE OUR ESCORT

As I lingered a moment in the ward-room, hating the thought of descending to my inferno, a member of the Prime Minister's suite came in and sat down beside me.

"He's actually going to bed," said he, with a happy smile. "I can hardly believe it. Now I can go to bed too! After a film he generally settles down to work half way through the night."

I saw relief on the worn face of the P.M.'s young man as he went off to his unaccustomed rest.

For the last hour or so—I had first noticed it during the final reel of the film—the battleship, which had been moving a bit all evening, showed a tendency to roll. Now the wind changed to a high scream and the *Prince of Wales* was lifted upon the crest of the Atlantic swell and held there a moment before she descended with a crash and a shudder. We were running into a gale. I stepped out upon the quarter-deck, but the wind was so powerful that I was unable to breathe and, turning my back to it, I was blown towards the rear gun turret, where I stood gasping for breath and holding to a steel cable. A shadowy figure stood there wearing an oilskin and muffled to the eyes.

"Much safer weather for us," he said. "The U-boats don't much care for this sort of thing!"

It was a dark night. The wind made a continuous high scream as it swept over the ship. I could see the quarter-deck lifting towards the sky and falling into the black pit of the sea. After a time I could make out the destroyers by the kicks of white spray in which they were plunging. They would become invisible for a long time, hidden by the swell, then I would see them far off, a clear spit of white as the seas broke over them.

I made a dash for the ward-room, grasped the black-out tarpaulin and found myself in warmth and light. The ship was now alarmingly active. With some difficulty, I descended ladders with the aid of inadequate hand ropes. I had to stand a moment in steel corridors, while the ship tilted, until she had righted herself again; and so, with sudden rushes, long pauses, perilous descents upon steel-shod steps, I found my way at last to the place where midshipmen were hanging in rows like brown cocoons. Bending almost double and skimming their unconscious forms with the top of my head, I gained the door of Cabin 27. It was not an easy journey. In war-time a battleship is closed-down at night. Familiar short cuts by day are shut by steel gates. Hatchways open by day are, by night, steel manholes through which one crawls with difficulty; and indeed the whole ship is subtly changed in appearance. Familiar landmarks, by means of which a stranger learns to find his way about, no longer exist or are replaced by such objects as lengths of fire-hose and other topographically misleading precautions.

I undressed on the Bismarckian bulge and climbed into my bunk, but sleep was out of the question. The noise was indescribable; the vibration so persistent that all my books, shaving things, hair brushes, and such like, had jumped to the cabin floor where they rolled a foot to port and a foot to starboard with the movement of the ship. The battleship descended into the seas like a falling lift, to rise with surprising buoyancy and slide forward before settling down into the water again. I had been to sea in big ships before, and I remember the old *Iron Duke*, the *Marlborough* and the *Rodney* in the Bay of Biscay, but I had never experienced such movement before, which I imagined was caused by the high speed at which we were travelling.

It has been my experience at sea that as long as you feel the rise and fall of a ship only across the forehead, you are never ill; but if you feel it in the stomach as well, you are sea-sick. This has fortunately never happened to me, either in big ships or in trawlers, but I am always expecting it to happen; and therefore I welcome the slight feeling of anæsthesia, as if some drug had been injected into the top of my skull.

The monstrous plunges of a great battleship are so deliberate and slow as to be unlike the movement of any other ship, indeed they are not like the movement of a ship at all: it is as though some vast steel works, or some factory like Cammel Lairds, were flying, unsteadily through the air. Almost as alarming as the movement are the sounds of a battleship in a storm; sounds to which the landsman can give no name and for which he can find no explanation: sudden bumps and bangs of ferocious power, as if the ship had struck a rock or had been kicked by a passing leviathan, followed by an uneasy silence in which metallic objects fall with a crash and men are heard far away running in heavy boots on steel decks.

I lay in electric light, with an electric fan turning, trying to read, envying the midshipmen outside in the alley who swung gently to the storm, maintaining the horizontal; and I wondered, too, how Mr. Churchill was getting on on the deck above me. Two parallel streaks of water, horrid ambassadors of the storm, entered beneath my cabin door and stole forward inch by inch. 1 lay watching them as they tried to reach my shoes, but always turning back just in time as the ship heeled and sent them racing under the door like a couple of black rats.

Two o'clock, three o'clock, half-past three; and I was still awake; then, chewing up some paper from my note-book and plugging my ears with the pulp, I managed to exclude some of the noise and I fell asleep, but for only half an hour. A bugle sounded. A fierce and mighty voice magnified by a loud speaker outside my cabin was chanting a queer couplet straight from the eighteenth century:—

> Heave-ho; Heave-ho, Heave-ho,
> Lash up and stow. . . .

How extraordinary it is that these steel fortresses should be haunted by Nelson. I climbed from my bunk and glanced outside where the midshipmen were tumbling from their hammocks lashing them up and stowing them away, as they had been commanded to do by the Voice. The Voice then ordered the ship to its action stations. I glanced at my watch: it was just after four o'clock. Dawn was breaking. I could hear the sound of feet above me, and from the length and breadth of the mighty ship, from every set of steel stairs, came the noise of feet running up on deck. I knew that above me the dawn "stand-to" was in progress; that urgent moment when a battleship scans the pale sea for any mast that may have crept up in the hours of darkness. Men were serving the great guns, the smaller guns, the chatter-guns that point their many mouths skywards and are known to sailors as Chicago Pianos because, thinks the Navy, if a gangster possessed an organ that is the kind of instrument he should have! Upon the bridge, and from other high places, men were gazing through field glasses at a segmented horizon; and the ship, greeting the dawn with mistrust, was ready for battle. The essence of self-preservation in the Navy is the readiness to send several tons of high explosive in a given direction a split second before several tons of high explosive are despatched from an apparently innocent sky-line.

Dressing was not too easy that morning. The water in the basin flowed first to one side, then to the other; hair brushes ran along the length of the locker and, cleverly evading my outstretched hand, fell on the cabin floor. The whole ship was shaking and shuddering; green mountains went hissing past the steel plates outside.

I went on deck and saw the ocean moving in pale hills and valleys striped in white. Astern lay our wake, a huge fading half-circle of cream; and I saw that we were zigzagging all the time. Then I noticed that our destroyers were no longer visible. There was no doubt about it. Our escort had vanished. Winston Churchill was alone on the Atlantic!

The first man I met in the ward-room, a red-eyed young man in a duffel coat who had just come off watch, told me that when we hit the storm on the previous night it was a question of reducing speed and retaining the destroyer screen or of maintaining speed and losing them. Speed was reduced to 18 knots in the hope that the destroyers would be able to maintain station, but this, owing to the heavy sea that was running, they were unable to do, and so we parted company at 1.5 a.m. and immediately put on speed, continuing on our way alone. If England could have known at that moment that the Prime Minister was bucketing about the Atlantic battleground unescorted by a single warship or aircraft, what would England have said? If Hitler could have known, what would Hitler have said?

"Will they catch up with us again?" I asked the officer.

"Not a hope," he replied. "We may get some destroyers from Iceland or somewhere, but they can't possibly reach us to-day."

In the early hours of that morning as we crossed the Atlantic alone the first excitement occurred, although few people were aware of it. A U-boat was reported, by what mysterious agency I cannot say, almost directly ahead of us. We altered course at once in order to avoid that sinister craft and did not resume our original course until 1.30 p.m.

Breakfast in a battleship is an amusingly misanthropic occasion. Talk is banned by common agreement. In order to make this clear to all, the Navy specialises in an anti-social device known as a magazine-stand. When erected in front of a plate of porridge and furnished with an ancient copy of the *Tatler*, this indicates to all beholders that the reader desires no contact with his fellow men.

But on the morning of Tuesday, August 5th, 1941, there was considerable conversation at breakfast in H.M.S. *Prince of Wales*, as she gambolled on her way to Newfoundland. It concerned the disappearance of Winston Churchill from his luxurious flat in the Admiral's quarters to the spartan surroundings of the Admiral's sea cabin on the bridge. This story was told with many first-hand details by the young gentleman who happened to be on watch at the time and was summoned to attend the removal.

It appeared that when the ship ran into the storm Mr. Churchill was preparing for bed. He noticed that objects were flung to the floor and that the noise was considerable, but, having slept through much noise in London within recent times, he thought he would give things a chance to improve and so retired to rest. But they did not improve: they became rapidly worse. It was then that the young officer, timidly entering the sacred regions, was faced by an angry and unconventionally attired Prime Minister. "He looked like an enraged cherub," said the young man.

The racket in the Admiral's quarters being, as the young man put it, "quite hellish," with the propellers coming out of the water now and then and "wagging the ship's tail," Mr. Churchill assumed his siren suit and demanded to be taken to the Admiral's sea cabin on the bridge. This was no easy undertaking in a blacked-out, closed-down ship. Even in daylight, with the ship at anchor, such a journey revives memories of a walk along Princes Street, Edinburgh. However, they set off, the officer leading, flashing a torch upon steel decks, casting a warning beam upon massive obstructions; and behind him the Prime Minister went softly through the sleeping ship.

At the end of the walk something equivalent to one of the towers of Westminster Abbey had to be ascended by

means of a number of ladders and short flights of steps leading from deck to deck and from stage to stage of the bridge.
The officer and the Prime Minister climbed one after the
other, some were easy, others were not so easy, because the
ship, having been closed for action, offered only a small,
man-hole instead of a generous hatchway; and into these
apertures; the Prime Minister introduced his reluctant figure. The young officer, who was apparently unaware that his
companion had been in a cavalry charge at Omdurman, had
been shot at by Cubans, Boers and Huns, had escaped from
prison in South Africa and had stolen rides on freight trains,
saw him only as a wilful elderly gentleman who must be
helped and protected. So, coming at last to the most treach-
erous stair of all, the ship rolling desperately, the young man
attempted to take the Prime Minister's arm. But he shrank
back into the shadows, and his torch went out, as he heard a
voice in the darkness say:

"Young man, do you imagine that I have never climbed
a ladder in my life?"

The young man was too awed to point out that this was
a very nasty ladder, and he waited with alarm for the moment
when the Prime Minister's head should come into contact
with four inches of solid steel.

"But, do you know," he said, describing the incident, "the
most extraordinary thing happened. I expected a proper
mouthful, but—*he never said a word*! I tell you, it was absolutely awe-inspiring."

In the course of the morning, we learned that Mr. Churchill
liked the Admiral's sea cabin so well that he had decided to
stay there throughout the voyage. He had also taken a fancy

to the Warrant Officers' Mess on the deck below the ward-
room, and this was hastily commandeered for him as a
sitting- and dining-room; so within twenty-four hours all
the official arrangements for his reception were changed.

It soon became known that a record had been broken.
Mr. Churchill had enjoyed his longest night's rest since the
war. His secretaries went through the ship like evangelists
spreading the glad tidings, and hoping that the record would
be maintained.

Those who expected to see Mr. Churchill striding about
the quarter-deck were disappointed. It was no day for such
activities. He spent the day on the bridge watching the
showers of spray whip over the fo'c'sle, and sometimes,
looking up, we saw him behind plate-glass wearing the siren
suit and smoking the often-dead cigar; for it is, of course,
obvious, that no human being could smoke as many cigars
as Mr. Churchill is reputed to do. To Mr. Churchill, a cigar is
a habit, almost a part of his attire, and sometimes he smokes
them and at other times they go out. Sometimes he relights
them, but more often than not he just forgets them and they
lie dead in his mouth until he suddenly flings them away.
His passion for cigars dates from the year 1895 when as a
young man of twenty, after eight months as a subaltern in
the 4th Hussars, he volunteered for the only war in progress
at that time and found himself in Cuba attached to the army
of General Campos. It was there, in Havana, that he encountered his life's companions.

Although Mr. Churchill was not always visible to the
ship, evidence of him was bellowed all over the battleship by
loud-speaker. Men in the engine room, sailors on the mess
decks, Marine sentries and others smiled with delight as

they heard unaccustomed orders shouted, such as "Will Mr. Martin please go at once to the Prime Minister on the bridge?" or "The Prime Minister requests the presence of Brigadier Dykes upon the bridge." Hearing such orders the crew caught a reflected glory and knew that this voyage was like no other.

I spent the afternoon in a welcome coma in a wardroom chair. When I awakened, Spring and some others were discussing a rumour that our voyage had become known in Germany. How this came to us, I do not know, whether by ship's wireless or whether Father Driscoll, the R.C. Chaplain, had been able to charm a word from the ward-room wireless set, a horrible machine possessed of a legion of electrical devils which the priest was always attempting to exorcise.

No one seemed in the least degree worried by this rumour, and one officer, as he casually flipped the pages of *Punch*, remarked that he supposed we would have to fight our way home. I asked a member of the party whether the Prime Minister had heard the rumour and, if so, what he had said about it. I was told that he had chuckled and twinkled and had been immensely amused.

"Between you and me," said this member of the party, "there's nothing he would like better than a bit of action."

A young officer looked up.

"By the way," he asked, "what happens to 'the Prime' if we go into action?"

"He goes below the armour-plate," replied a senior officer sternly.

"Well, that may be the rule," said the member of the party with a laugh, "but I wouldn't like to be the man who ordered him to go down there. I know where he *would* be in action—on the bridge!"

Spring and I wondered what the effect would be could we cable the story into any newspaper office in England or the States that Winston Churchill was in the North Atlantic unescorted by a single destroyer.

The Engineer-Commander looked up from his paper.

"I suppose that's what would be called a scoop," he remarked solemnly.

We thought that might possibly describe it.

We attended "the P.M.'s" second film show that evening. The procedure was the same as upon the previous night. The Prime Minister came in. We rose to our feet. He bowed towards us. We sat down and the room was thrown into darkness. But this night, instead of the film we had expected to see, something different flickered across the screen, and a few cynics whispered that the ship's operator had got a bit mixed up. We saw an aeroplane coming down on a foreign air-field. Military officers and officials rushed up to it, the door of the plane opened and—Mr. Harry Hopkins stepped out.

Mr. Churchill roared with approval.

"Oh, there you are, Harry!" he shouted. "Bravo! Bravo!" and he clapped his hands with pleasure.

And Mr. Hopkins, who had produced this brief glimpse of his recent flight to Russia as a surprise for Mr. Churchill, sat there delighted too. It was an episodic film, just a number of stray shots showing Mr. Hopkins arriving here and leaving there, guards presenting arms, military lorries moving along roads and that sort of thing. But it was, at its first showing, what is known in the film world as a smash hit. There was no doubt about it that, for one evening at least, Mr. Hopkins was Mr. Churchill's favourite film star.

During the intervals, while the reels were being changed, gramophone records were played over a loud speaker. Mr. Churchill asked if any officer in the ship had a record of Noel Coward's "Mad Dogs and Englishmen." This was produced, and Mr. Churchill proved that he knew the words and the tune. The other side of the record was the toast, "To England," from *Cavalcade*. When the last words were spoken, the hope that England might live in dignity and peace, there was no sound in the ward-room but a deep, emotional "Hear, hear!" from Mr. Churchill. Another record in which the Prime Minister was also word perfect was a foxtrot called "Franklin D. Roosevelt Jones."

When the show was over, Mr. Churchill, smoking a cigar of a size recognised by the gunnery officer as "a fifteen-incher," bowed gracefully and retired on a tidal wave of benevolence.

VI

THE MAP ROOM

On Wednesday, August 6th, the storm had died away. A white fog, which someone said was blowing off the Newfoundland Banks, shrouded the sea, and into this we moved with undiminished speed. It was cold and a trifle clammy; and the sight of the mighty battleship, hardly able to see ahead more than her own length yet steaming at full speed, was impressive, even thrilling. It was a happy morning for U-boats: calm, foggy, a perfect morning to surface and take a shot, and the speed of our ship, combined with our erratic course, proved that those upon our bridge had no illusions.

We had been travelling without an escort since Monday night, our first night at sea, and now upon Wednesday, we had news that three Canadian-manned destroyers from Iceland were to pick us up and take us on to Placentia Bay. How we were able to wireless our position to them—information which presumably was one of the greatest secrets of the moment—I cannot imagine; but that we had done so was made clear at 11.30 a.m., when the snapping signal lamps upon our bridge were answered by quick sparks of Morse from the fog ahead. For the second time since leaving Scapa, we reduced speed a little as three grey shapes came out of the fog, three destroyers, *Ripley*, *Restigouche*, and *Assiniboine*. They fell into position ahead and abeam of us, our turbines quickened, and we plunged on into the fog.

When I met the Prime Minister on deck in the afternoon, I was surprised to notice a change in his appearance. Gaiety and buoyancy are a part of his nature, and they break through even when he is most exhausted; but now, so much good had the rest done him, that he was not only sprightly but, there is no other word for it, boyish; and not a very good little boy either. As I walked beside him on the quarter-deck I remembered that a schoolmistress in Brighton had described him, at the age of eight, as "a small, red-headed pupil, the naughtiest boy in the class," and I was on the point of telling him a story I had heard about him only a week or so before when I was travelling in a train from Farnham to London. The only other person in the carriage was a dowager of a type now rapidly becoming extinct. She had a mass of beautiful white hair, the face of an eighteenth-century general, and she sat bolt upright in the carriage as if she were in a brougham. She asked me if I had listened to the Prime Minister on the previous Sunday, and what did I think of his broadcast.

"Whenever I listen to the Prime Minister," she said, "I remember something that happened when I was a small girl. I was taken once a year to stay in Brown's Hotel in Albemarle Street.

"My governess used to tell me stories of an exceedingly naughty little boy who took his meals in the servants' hall downstairs. He was small and fat and red-headed, and he was also greedy. He used to play all kinds of tricks upon the dig-nified ladies' maids and valets—such as sticking pins in their

President Roosevelt leaning on the arm of his son, Captain Elliott Roosevelt, as he stepped aboard the *Prince of Wales* on Sunday, August 10th, 1941

Mr. Churchill restrains the ship's cat from boarding the
President's destroyer

chairs and making booby-traps for them—and, in particular, upon the housekeeper herself. This little boy's name was Winston Churchill. My governess was shocked by him and she used to tell me stories about him with a moral purpose, in order, of course, to underline the polite virtues. She failed dismally. While the wicked Winston Churchill was performing these crimes in the servants' hall downstairs, a little girl used to sit upstairs in a drawing-room and long to see such a bad boy. But I never managed to see him. And now, when I hear our dear Prime Minister on the wireless, my mind goes back over all those years to Brown's Hotel in Albemarle Street. . . ."

And as I looked at Winston Churchill's mischievous eyes that afternoon, it occurred to me that the naughty little boy of Brown's Hotel is still there, playing hide-and-seek, and ready for any adventure. He is liable to bob up at any moment and stick a pin in a chair, incalculable, provoking, ingenious, and guaranteed always to produce a sense of violent irritation in more elderly rigid natures. Some essential part of Winston has refused to surrender to age.

It is, perhaps, that part of him which is sensed by crowds in picture theatres, who laugh with delight when they see him waving from the hood of a taxi, or holding his hat on a walking-stick—for Winston has always had a juvenile love for wearing comic hats—and when they observe him twinkling merrily at some parade or pausing wickedly to make that gesture which in England has not always meant V for Victory, they express an affection for him which they could never feel for an entirely grown-up, dried-up human being. Who but an extremely naughty little boy would have dared to call Mussolini Hitler's "utensil"? It is this provocative, authentic touch of naughtiness in Winston that rouses both curiosity and affection, and so it happens that, after a lifetime spent amid the violent hatred and suspicion of his peers, he has become at last by the irony of fate and by virtue of his own great qualities, the best-loved statesman in the recent history of England.

The Prime Minister spent his day conferring with the Chiefs of Staff, dictating correspondence and discussing his forthcoming meeting with the President. After luncheon he retired as usual to bed. This he does every day. And when he goes to bed he undresses, gets in between the sheets and goes to sleep. He has himself stated that "when I was at the Admiralty in the War, I found I could add nearly two hours to my working effort by going to bed for an hour after luncheon."

This habit has been traced to Cuba by Mr. Philip Guedella, in his book *Mr. Churchill*. Not only did Mr. Churchill encounter the cigar in Cuba when he was serving as a soldier there when a young man of twenty, but he also, according to Mr. Guedella, readily adopted the Spanish custom of going to bed in the afternoon. On the other hand, Sir Edward Marsh, who was often Mr. Churchill's private secretary, dates this habit only from the 1914–18 War, and traces it to his own example. "We began the day about nine o'clock," says Sir Edward in *A Number of People*, describing his life when Mr. Churchill was First Lord of the Admiralty in 1914, "and went on usually till one or two next morning. . . . Luncheon was a bite at my club in Whitehall Gardens, followed by a twenty minutes' nap, and when I told Winston of this he laughed at me for a dormouse; but one day something impelled him to try it himself, and it answered so well that thenceforward he got right into bed for about an hour every afternoon."

After his sleep, the Prime Minister, full of renewed energy, would generally pay a visit to the Map Room to see what was happening.

The Map Room in the *Prince of Wales* was a replica in miniature of the famous Map Room at the Admiralty. It had been fitted up on the Prime Minister's instructions by two officers from the Admiralty, Captain Pim and Lieut.-Commander McMullen. They had taken over an office in the ship for the purpose. An enormous map of the Atlantic Ocean occupied one wall. It was lit by strip lights. The opposite wall bore large maps of the Russian front. The officers in charge were busily engaged all day in filing war cables and marking up the maps to correspond with them. The position of every ship, warships and merchant ships alike, and the position of every known U-boat, were plotted hour by hour upon the huge map of the Atlantic Ocean. The U-boats were represented by sinister little coffin-shaped ebony pins; enemy aircraft by black T's; warships were grey; merchant ships were red. Most impressive to see were the great convoys crossing the Atlantic, sixty and seventy little red ships escorted by grey ships lying in a wide space of open water. One immediately looked round for the nearest U-boat. There they were, sometimes a pack of six little black coffins, but well away to north or south. The convoy was safe for the moment!

Captain Pim would read a message, bring it over to the map, work out the longitude and latitude, and quietly place a couple of black coffins in the path of the convoy. It was difficult to realise that this was real, that this was happening all about us at that moment, that it was not some exciting game of chance or skill. And, as I looked at the ever-moving picture of the Battle of the Atlantic, translating it in my mind from a purely academic problem on a map into terms of human life and death, of ships, men and munitions, I prayed that those convoys and their escorts knew, as we knew, of the black coffins in their path. Sometimes a great moment came when I was fortunate enough to be in the room, and the thrill of it is not easily to be forgotten. Captain Pim would rise from his chair with a message in his hand. He would come over to the map, calculate for a moment and then remove a U-boat.

"Destroyed," he would say in a passionless voice and throw the coffin pin into a tray. It was superbly final.

All day long the ships on this map were moving, homeward or outward. It was interesting to follow the fortunes of, say, a convoy approaching England. At ten o'clock in the morning it would be nearing port with two or three black coffins round about it; then at two o'clock it would have moved nearer port, the coffins perhaps in the same position, then, if you were lucky enough to return at the right moment, you might see Captain Pim pick sixty or seventy little red boats from the map and drop them in the tray. The convoy had got through!

The position of the *Prince of Wales* on this map was, of course, of outstanding interest. I often went in to find out where we were and also to look for the nearest U-boat; and some seemed to me quite near enough! Delighted on one such occasion to see the death of a U-boat, I said to Captain Pim.

"Has that U-boat been sunk?"

A well-known voice behind took me to task. Winston Churchill had quietly entered the Map Room.

"Only British submarines are sunk," he said with a smile. "German U-boats are—*destroyed*!"

And the amount of venom he put into the word "destroyed," which he expelled from his mouth as if he had been chewing coke, giving to the word the same rising intonation heard over the wireless when he speaks of that "Wicked Man," was truly terrific.

The film that evening was *The Devil and Miss Jones* an American comedy which did not impress all of us. But Mr. Churchill sat through it with every sign of pleasure. He had come intending to enjoy himself, and he was determined to do so. He appeared to lose himself completely in the sentimental adventures of a New York shop assistant, and I thought that his gift of switching his mind from the important to the trivial, and, moreover, giving the trivial his undivided attention, is a gift to be envied. It is interesting to watch someone who knows the secret of complete relaxation.

VII

A BATTLESHIP IN WAR-TIME

On Thursday, August 7th, I explored the *Prince of Wales*.

I climbed, by means of perpendicular iron ladders, into remote control positions where I came upon young men in brown duffel coats sitting before a bewildering array of instruments: dials, clocks, handles, levers, bell-pushes and the like. That is modern war. The pilot's seat in a bomber is not unlike the inside of a gun-control turret. It is a place where, on the principle of ringing for afternoon tea and with no greater effort, a young man can pull a lever or press a button and send several tons of high explosive into the sky. The labour-saving devices of Death are remarkable. While Nelson's seamen, stripped naked to the waist, man-handled their tethered guns and lit them with fire, the modem gunner picks up a telephone, receives his orders and presses a button. No more physical effort is involved in firing a broadside from the *Prince of Wales* than in ringing the vicarage bell.

In such a control, fanned by a warm breath from the funnels, I encountered four cheerful young men. The huge ship lay dizzily below like a model in Basset-Lowke's, stretching grey and neat as she thrust her way through the sea. Two of the young men had been through both the River Plate and the *Bismarck* actions, but they had no readily accessible memories of either. It is astounding how much youth can forget. They were laughing, cheerful boys, oddly monk-like in their hooded coats; but no monk ever had such wicked blue eyes. They told me that the *Bismarck* "show" was a bit of bad luck because they were called off just when they wanted to go on fighting; still the *Tirpitz* was afloat and they looked forward to having a crack at her one day.

They described to me what they could remember of their own feelings as the ship went into action with the *Bismarck*; but anyone could invent more exciting impressions of a sea battle without joining the Navy. Few of the ship's company ever saw the *Bismarck*. They were below decks at their duties or enclosed in steel turrets dependent for information upon the Captain's broadcasts from the bridge. They thought highly of their Captain for keeping them in touch with events.

"We were waiting the order to fire," said one young man. "We knew it would come at any moment and we were ready. Then, instead of the order, we heard the Padre reading a prayer. But we got the order to fire soon after."

I had already heard that story from the Chaplain, the Rev. W. G. Parker. Just before action was joined he was called to the bridge by Captain Leach.

"Padre, we are going into action," said the Captain, and we shall need help. I want you to read a prayer to the ship's company. Can you remember that prayer, which begins, 'O, God, thou knowest how busy I am . . .'?"

"Yes, sir," replied the Padre. "It's called Sir Jacob Astley's prayer before Edgehill, and I have the words in my cabin."

"Go, then, and fetch it quickly," said the Captain, "There's not much time."

While the battleship, steaming into action, was taut with expectancy, every nerve stretched to meet the explosion of the fourteen-inch guns, instead of the order to fire there came to every corner of the ship, from engine-room to crow's nest, the sound of the Chaplain's voice, saying:

"O Lord, Thou knowest how busy we must be to-day, if we forget Thee, do not Thou forget us; for Christ's sake. Amen."

Then the guns fired.

War brings to a soldier complete alteration in the everyday details of his life. He wears perhaps a different uniform, he changes his quarters, maybe his weapons are new or he is taught to use them differently; he may find himself in a strange country among men who do not speak his language and, indeed, his attitude to war is adaptation to changed, and ever-changing, conditions.

With a sailor it is different. He fights in what are his barracks and his home. His ship in peace-time is theoretically already prepared for war, ready to repel or deliver an attack. Thus the change over from peace to war hardly affects the daily routine of his life at all. It might be a sweeping generalisation to say, though there is some truth in it, that in a battleship the outward difference between peace and war is the end of spit and polish and the beginning of action stations. In war a ship is even encouraged to become tarnished, her decks are no longer made to shine like satin and the energy released is used in other directions.

Still, apart from dawn and dusk action stations and frequent alarms, the sight of every sailor in a Mae West and the blacking-out and closing-down at night, there was little to indicate that the *Prince of Wales* was at war. There were long periods of the day when she might well have been cruising in peace-time. The same bugles summoning cooks and mess orderlies, the call for Captain's Requestmen, the rum ration bugles, and other daily features of a life at sea, proved that the domestic life of the battleship was in smooth, unaltered progress.

In the ward-room, too, as in peace-time, the same limp forms snatched a sleep between watches, the same figures solemnly read an antique number of *The Illustrated London News*, the same silent breakfasts were eaten, the same innocuous pink gins circulated before dinner. Yet in the twinkling of an eye the scene could change. An alarm upon the ship's siren would send feet clattering up iron stairs, the ward-room would empty in a flash, steel doors would be shut; while on deck sailors in steel helmets would stand to the A.A. guns and in a sinister silence the fourteen-inch turrets would smoothly swing round and the big guns would nose the sky.

I was delighted to see that the parade, "Up Spirits," is still carried on sharp at eleven o'clock in war as in peace. The same rum-bound dignitaries descend into the spirit store, taking with them the bucolic little rum pump and the same careful rationing is performed, as if each fraction of a drop of rum were a distillation of the Koh-i-noor. The spirit is diluted with water and put to rest in a great loyal cask of oak, which bears the words *The King, God Bless Him*, in brass letters, and then a long file of mess orderlies with tins and pannikins waits to distribute the grog to the consumers.

Surgeon-Commander Quinn took me to a parade which he thought would interest me, called Captain's Requestmen. It is the Naval equivalent of a C.O.'s orderly-room in the

Army. It was held in the Marine Barracks, a large open space
on one of the lower decks. Those members of the ship's
company with a request to make stood in rows facing an
officer, who represented the Captain. They came up one by
one, doffed their caps and stood to attention while they
made their requests. Most requested, that allowances should
be transferred from mothers to wives. There were also some
puzzling requests. One man stepped up and said:

"Permission to grow, sir."

This did not make much sense to me, and I thought that
I had probably not heard the man properly, but when a second and a third expressed the same unspecified ambition I
whispered to Quinn:

"Request to grow what?"

"A beard," he whispered back.

It appears that no beard may be grown in the Navy without the Captain's permission. That is to prevent the beard
trivial, the beard temporary, but, above all, the beard spuri-
ous, and the beard which is no beard at all, but merely an
indication of the wearer's dislike for shaving. Once "permission to grow" has been granted, a razor must not from that
moment be used without official permission, and the beard
must remain *in situ*, no matter what the owner's friends and
shipmates may say and think about it, for a period of three
calendar months. If at the end of that time the beard is not
popular, and some splendid growths are being continually
sacrificed to the whims of women, the man may appear
again before the Captain and be granted permission to shave.
The number of men who look like an advertisement for
Navy Cut, the result of three months' intensive cultivation,
then go on leave and, having come in contact with wives

and sweethearts, return to their ships and ask permission to become smooth-faced again, proves that beards are not popular with Englishwomen. There have been instances of men who look like rabbits in the ordinary way, having been transformed by beards into Francis Drakes; yet this has no effect on their womenfolk: they just don't like it; and a bronzed and hairy hero is forced by these Delilahs to revert to a chinless mediocrity.

I paid a visit to the bakery, where one thousand five hundred loaves of white flour are baked every day; to the kitchens, still quaintly called the galley, where electrical ovens and every kind of aluminium device challenges comparison with the kitchens of the Ritz, and to a canteen stocked ceiling-high with chocolate at less than pre-war prices and with all kinds of cigarettes, which I thought were practically given away. I descended, clothed in a suit of dungarees, to the engine-room, where, in the temperature of Trinidad and in a vast cathedral of asbestos-covered pipes, engineers stood watching dials and measuring distilled water like so many chemists. The turbines throbbed while the great propeller shafts, revolving in yellow grease, thundered in the darkness. Ascending with relief to more temperate regions, I was in time to be present at one of those domestic interludes which enliven the existence of a battleship, even in war-time.

Three Marines were holding three cats. They held them not as animal lovers, but as soldiers, as if cats were part of their equipment, as if, indeed, they might be ordered to "for inspection, port cats!"; which is precisely what they were doing. An officer came along and, having scrutinised the cats, solemnly dismissed them.

I was told the explanation. When the *Prince of Wales* returned from the shipyard after a brief refitment following the *Bismarck* action, a peculiar smell was noticed on one of the decks. This smell, increasing in volume and pungency, inspired two schools of thought: one, that the shipwrights had used some unusually penetrating glue or other material, the other, that one of the ship's three cats had chosen an inaccessible hiding-place in which to expire. It was therefore decided to muster the cats and solve at least one of the theories which, as I saw, was happily unfounded.

Until her visit to the shipyard, I was told, the *Prince of Wales* prided herself on her ratlessness. But when she returned to duty a few rats had come aboard and action was immediately taken. It was proclaimed that any sailor who caught a rat would earn half a day ashore, and this made the life of a rat in the *Prince of Wales* a brief and hazardous affair. The business was arranged with the usual naval precision. Rats having been caught, the trappers were required to parade with them. An inspecting officer cynically remained until he had seen the rats faithfully destroyed. Then the trappers were able to qualify for their reward. I asked if anyone had thought it worth while to import such desirable quarry but I was answered with a stony and disapproving stare.

The Prime Minister had been invisible all day. I asked a member of his staff what he had been doing. I was told that he had held the usual war meeting in company with the Chiefs of Staff, as if he were at home in Downing Street. He had received a stream of telegrams from the Admiralty, the War Office and other State departments. He had kept in touch with every development of the War on land, at sea and on the home front. He had dictated letters and instructions, and had sent off a string of telegrams, and he had studied the boxes of State papers which he had brought with him dealing with all aspects of the War.

"He has devised a working day," I was told, "and the less you see of him, the busier he will be."

That night an event of some moment occurred at the Prime Minister's table. Mr. Hopkins produced a jar of caviare which he had brought from Russia. The rumour in the ward-room was that Stalin had sent it as a gift to Mr. Churchill, but that was, of course, too perfect to be true. The simple truth was that Mr. Hopkins thought it was exceptionally good caviare and decided to buy it.

The film that evening was *High Sierra*, a highly-coloured affair with plenty of shooting. When the gangster villain had been finally run to earth and had rolled dead from rock to rock down a mountain-side, Mr. Churchill remarked, "And a good time was had by all!" So, bowing, cigar in hand, he left us.

VIII

A REHEARSAL

It was now Friday, August 8th, and we were due to anchor off the Newfoundland coast on the following morning at about nine o'clock. An air of excitement and anticipation filled the ship. We were all conscious that events of spectacular importance were soon to unfold themselves.

For Spring and myself the day brought disappointment. It was discovered that the President was coming to the meeting unaccompanied by his usual Pressmen, an unheard of proceeding even, it appears, when the President goes on a private fishing holiday. Naturally our hasty inclusion in the party, while it may have reflected credit upon the enterprise of the Minister of Information, was not likely to find much favour with the excluded members of the American Press. In the interests of harmony it was therefore decided that we should write nothing for immediate publication, that we should confine our observations to the happenings in our own ship and that we should not meet the President or visit any of the American ships. We readily accepted our novel status as a couple of literary stowaways with good grace, and we offered to write anything of a character sufficiently colourless and anonymous to meet the needs of a delicate situation. In the course of my career as a journalist I have been obliged to keep many important secrets, but I cannot remember having such a story to tell yet being unable to tell it. If we had been cast adrift in a ship's boat it might have been easier to bear, but to be present, to see the whole thing and yet to remain silent was going to be desperately hard. Spring is much more of a philosopher. He managed to extract quite a lot of gloomy enjoyment from the situation.

A rehearsal of President Roosevelt's reception was held in the *Prince of Wales* during the afternoon. The band of the Royal Marines, with a guard of honour, was posted on the starboard side of the quarter-deck. Sir Alexander Cadogan had been elected President. He stood rather shyly against the guard rail and lifted his hat to indicate that he had come aboard, whereupon the band played *The Star Spangled Banner*, the guard presented arms and Mr. Churchill walked up and shook hands, followed by the Chiefs of Staff. The ship's officers then advanced in single file into an extremely cold and violent wind, saluting and giving an "eyes right" to the "President" as they came level with him.

Mr. Churchill, with cigar, wearing a yachting cap and a navy blue suit with a double-breasted jacket and brass buttons, stood apart, criticising and frequently stopping the proceedings from time to time. His faithful attendant, Inspector Thompson, who was standing near, growled angrily.

"Just look at him! Fancy standing in this wind without his overcoat. He'll get his death of cold."

And the thoughtful detective disappeared and returned with Mr. Churchill's overcoat. The rehearsal continued for a long time, until such time in fact that Mr. Churchill thought that the "President" had been adequately received; then the Marines marched away and the party broke up.

We met after dinner for the nightly film in a mood of great cheerfulness. Firstly, we were all excited by the thought of what the morrow held for us; secondly, the film was *Lady Hamilton*, which we had been told was so good that Mr. Churchill had already seen it four times.

The lights went out and the story of Nelson and Emma Hamilton was unfolded in a manner that might not perhaps have satisfied an historian, but was satisfying to the emotions. Imagine the scene. We were in the ward-room of a battleship at sea and the audience was composed of officers who had recently taken the ship into action. As in Nelson's day, England was again at war, fighting for her life. Sitting in the front row in the light of the screen was a man no longer young in years whose worst enemy has never been able to say that he has ever faltered in his love for England, a man who, after a life of violent political hostility, has come at last, without rancour for prophesies unheeded or advice despised, to lead England to victory. The story he watched was one that touched his heart: the story of a man who gave everything he had to give so that England might live in freedom and in peace.

Winston Churchill was completely absorbed in the story, and for the first time spoke no longer to those near him, but seemed to retreat into himself, as if he were sitting alone in the dark, his face, his body even, expressing an attention so complete that it seemed one might look and find him no longer there, but taken up, merged and absorbed by the screen. Children wish themselves into picture-books and go riding with Red Cross knights, fighting dragons and blowing horns at castle gates, with that same passionate intensity of feeling and imagination. But it is rare to encounter it in disenchanted men. Then, as the last scene came, and Nelson lay dying in the cock-pit of the *Victory*, and they bent above him and told him that the day was his, the man who was watching so intently took a handkerchief from his pocket and wiped his eyes without shame.

It is only within the last two hundred years that Englishmen have become ashamed of tears. Our forefathers were not ashamed to weep openly, and the references to tears in the literature of England prove to us that, to the men of other days, a man incapable of tears was believed to be a man hard, inhuman and inaccessible to mercy. Looking at Winston Churchill at that revealing moment, I thought that in some extraordinary way he belongs definitely to an older England, to the England of the Tudors, a violent swashbuckling England perhaps, but a warm and emotional England too, an England as yet untouched by the hardness of an age of steel.

I have sometimes studied the effect of Churchill's voice and words upon an ordinary gathering of men in a public-house. Why, I have wondered, should they have been so firmly held, so silent until the last word? And I have wondered if it may not be that he speaks with the voice of an older England, that we recognise the voice, not of an industrialist, but of one who has, so to speak, missed the Industrial Revolution and speaks to us as if from the deck of the *Golden Hind*. Churchill's voice is also classless. He has no public school accent. Like the Elizabethans, he speaks not as an Etonian but as an Englishman.

President Roosevelt and Mr. Churchill on the quarter-deck of
the *Prince of Wales* after the church parade service,
Sunday, August 10th, 1941

The Anglo-American church parade on the quarter-deck of the *Prince of Wales*, Sunday, August 10th. Mr. Churchill, the President and the Chiefs of the British and American Staffs are seated to the left of the picture facing the guns

As I watched him wipe the tears from his eyes, I remembered that Sir Henry Wilson described that, during a black time in the last war, when he went to say good-bye to Winston on his way to France, the First Lord—as he then was—took his hand and said that he was sure he would lead to victory; then, unable to finish the sentence, broke down. And Wilson, an icy soldier, made this surprising comment: "I never liked him so much."

In Winston Churchill runs that deep current of feeling that ran through the Elizabethans, through men like Wolfe and Nelson, but stopped short at Wellington. And I think no one can deny that there is no other man living to-day in England, nor has there been for a hundred years, who could say in a moment of tragedy, "Kiss me, Hardy," without making us feel embarrassed. But Winston Churchill could do so because his roots go down into the body of that old, warm, emotional England. Therein may lie his power and his spell.

The lights went up. We were all, I think, intensely moved in our different ways. Mr. Churchill stood facing us, but this time he did not smile, bow and depart. He spoke in a grave and quiet voice, so quiet that those at the back of the room had to listen carefully to catch his words.

"I thought this would interest you, gentlemen," he said, "many of whom have been recently engaged with the enemy in matters of equal historical importance. Good night!"

"Good night, sir!"

He bowed and went out.

IX

THE COUNCIL OF PLACENTIA

THE great day had come at last. It was Saturday, 9th August.

Once the bugles had awakened me at the dawn stand-to, I was unable to sleep again. Wearing an overcoat over pyjamas, I went on deck anxious to catch the first glimpse of land. It was a cold, grey morning. The wind had dropped and the sea was calm. Still there was no sight of land. Becoming tired of pacing the quarter-deck, I thought I would go up to the Admiral's Bridge, my favourite vantage point, and always deserted at that time in the morning.

I had been standing there a few moments, watching the ship cleave her way through the water, when a door opened and Mr. Churchill came out wearing his siren suit and smoking the first of the day's cigars.

"Can you see any sign of them yet?" he asked eagerly, as he looked out to sea. I asked what he was looking for. "The American destroyers," he replied. We crossed from port to starboard of the bridge, but no ship was in sight: a calm sea stretched to the edge of the sky.

Chiefs of Staff, secretaries and attendants were still in their beds on that important morning, but the Prime Minister, eager and restless as a boy, was up and longing for the first sight of the Stars and Stripes. It was an interesting glimpse of him, and if in the future an historian wishes to describe him at that moment, he must picture the grey ship stained with the seas, striped with camouflage, her guns pointing forward in the stillness of the morning; no one about but a few sailors at their stations, and no sound but the hiss of water against her plates as she steamed through the quiet sea. High on the Admiral's Bridge, not in the steel and plate-glass bridge itself, but on the outside platform, stood Churchill on the eve of his mission. Just out of bed, his sandy hair still ruffled from the pillow, he stood watching the sea that stretched to the New World. In a few hours ceremony and anthems would begin, but in that quiet opening of the day, like a warrior awakened from his tent, he stood unarmed at dawn, surveying the scene, wondering maybe what the day would bring forth.

The War had provided no picture quite like that. We had seen the Dictators stepping from their armoured trains in the Brenner Pass, marching stiffly in military uniforms, their faces set in calculated scowls, but here was England's leader at the end of a hazardous voyage—which he had treated as though it were a pleasure cruise—alone, unspectacular, wearing the garment he had worn through London's most hideous nights.

I had no idea what was to be discussed or decided between Roosevelt and Churchill; but I had no doubt that it would be one of the significant meetings in history, and I thought that I should always remember the picture of Churchill just out of bed that morning, anxious to be the first to greet the American Navy.

★ ★ ★

We made contact with the American destroyers at 7.30 a.m. They came steaming towards us flying the Stars and Stripes. Mr. Churchill, in his blue semi-naval uniform, stood at the salute as they came up to us. We slowed down to enable an officer to board us from the American destroyer, *McDougal*. He told us of the berthing arrangements and we then realised that, because the American ships were not keeping the local Newfoundland Summer Time we were an hour and a half ahead of American time. We were not expected until 9 a.m. and we had arrived at 7.30! We therefore turned away and steamed off the coast for a while until the moment arrived for our entrance. Turning, and led by the American destroyers, we approached the entrance to Placentia Bay, which was now visible in the distance.

We saw ahead of us the outline of a grey and lonely land, a low silhouette of hills touched with mist; a land that seemed to us to bear a strong likeness to the isles we had left six days previously. Placentia Bay is one of the largest anchorages in the New World, and the greatest bay of many which cut into the southeastern corner of Newfoundland and give to that indented peninsula the shape of a star-fish. The entrance to the bay is fifty-five miles in width, and its waters penetrate for a distance of ninety miles into the land.

As the battleship steamed towards that wide inland sea, perhaps no more eager voyagers have ever gazed towards the shores of Newfoundland than those who stood together on the morning of Saturday, August the ninth, upon the bridge of the *Prince of Wales*. The Chiefs of Staff in their naval, military and Air Force uniforms, with their attendants and advisers, stood there with Mr. Churchill. The great battleship with the White Ensign flying in the morning breeze, followed the Stars and Stripes as they sped before us to the anchorage.

The land now became more clearly visible. Some of us who a week previously had anticipated perhaps a visit to New York and a progress along Broadway under a shower of ticker tape, contrasted that prospect with the desolate scene that now presented itself. We saw a wavering coast-line of desolate little beaches and coves, behind which the country rose in mournful hills clothed to the top with dense woods of fir and larch. It looked to me like perfect Red Indian country, the kind of country I had encountered so often in my youth in the pages of Fennimore Cooper. There were the same thick woods, the same lonely estuaries on whose placid waters trappers should have been paddling birch-bark canoes; but there was not a living soul to be seen, not one human dwelling, not one spiral of smoke from house or camp fire, nothing but primeval hills and the sea.

Rounding a promontory and entering the mouth of the bay, we saw at a glance the inspiring sight of the American warships waiting for us. They lay at anchor in the lee of land, some little distance from shore. Instantly from bridge and crow's nest in the *Prince of Wales* there occurred that sharp excitement of recognition which always takes place when warships meet at sea. Telescopes were levelled, and in a few seconds we knew them all by name. There, in the centre, was the cruiser *Augusta* with the President aboard; over there was the cruiser *Tuscaloosa*, and there—with her trelliswork main foremast rising like a small Eiffel Tower—lay the battleship *Arkansas*. The smaller ships that dotted the wide anchorage were a flotilla of destroyers. As we came in American seaplanes circled over us.

The *Prince of Wales* came steaming behind her American escort through a lane of ships that would bring her abreast of the *Augusta*. As we approached the President's cruiser we saw that an awning had been erected upon her forward gun turret. Beneath it stood a group of men in uniform, and in the centre was a tall man who wore a light brown suit. Through field glasses the whole scene leapt forward into life. Mr. Roosevelt, wearing a Palm Beach suit, was watching our approach, scrutinising us for the first sight of Mr. Churchill, just as Mr. Churchill was at that moment looking for him. Now and again the President would smile and turn to say something to one of the officers near him. Then, as we drew abreast, I saw him remove his hat and stand in salute as the *Prince of Wales* went by.

At that same moment Mr. Churchill was standing to attention on the quarter-deck, his hand raised to the peak of his cap. The bosuns' pipes shrilled. The crew stood to attention, and the band of the Royal Marines crashed into *The Star Spangled Banner*. Like an echo across the strip of water came the notes of *God Save the King*. So we passed to our anchorage where a flag on a buoy rose above the water. For a moment it seemed that we might cut it down, then, at the moment of touching it, the *Prince of Wales* slowed and stopped and, with a great noise, our anchor chains descended into Newfoundland fathoms. We had arrived in Placentia Bay upon the stroke of nine.

It soon became known that Mr. Churchill and the Chiefs of Staff would leave the ship at eleven o'clock to meet the President in the *Augusta*.

Meanwhile, a lot was happening. Gangways were being lowered. Motor boats, speed cutters, naval pinnaces, even a whaler, were swung out from our decks and lowered to the water. Soon the silence of Placentia Bay was shattered by the explosions of speed boats as small naval craft dotted the sea around us, some flying the Stars and Stripes, some the White Ensign. They moved between the British and American flotillas with an air of delightful animation and cheerfulness; and it was amusing to observe that the curiosity written upon the faces of British sailors when they approached an American ship was reflected in the faces of the Americans when they came near us.

We were a remarkable contrast as we lay anchored side by side. The *Prince of Wales* was camouflaged; her guns protruded from their turrets like rigid pythons. The American ships were uncamouflaged and shone in peace-time grey. We had been in action, and our brass was either painted or tarnished, and our decks were not what they would have been in other days. The American ships were spotless. We admired the beautiful rubber steps of their pinnaces, the gleaming brass, the pine-white woodwork, as those craft lay tossing in our grim shadow. It was almost with a shock that, having lived since 1939 in a country at war, I looked—as over a great gulf of experience—at such evidence of a country at peace.

Now and again, as some officer of rank ascended our gangway, the bosun would blow his pipe. Those within hearing would freeze into attention while the visitor saluted the quarter-deck, and, then, at the note of a bugle, they would relax and go about their tasks.

While I was watching these incidents, I met a strange naval officer upon the quarter-deck—a tall, elegant figure in captain's uniform, striding in solitary state with a

telescope under his arm. He had that definite air of owner-
ship which captain's assume upon their own quarter-decks.
He was Captain Leach, who had been invisible from the
moment of our sailing. He told me that he had been on the
bridge for six days and nights, and was now properly shaved
and clothed for the first time since leaving Scapa Flow. I
said something about the responsibility of taking Winston
Churchill across the Atlantic in war-time, and I received in
reply an eloquent glance of tired blue eyes, and a weary but
contented smile.

I mentioned how much I would like to set foot ashore
and explore some of the desolate little beaches which we
could see from the ship.

"That is impossible," he said. "I'm sorry, but my orders
are that no one may leave the ship."

To cross the Atlantic and see Newfoundland, yet not to
set foot ashore, was indeed a bitter disappointment. It did
not seem to be the luckiest day of my life.

At eleven o'clock Mr. Churchill appeared on deck with the
Chiefs of Staff. Glancing across at the *Augusta* I noticed that
the Americans were regrouped beneath the awning. The
President was in the centre with his officers around him.
The bosun's pipe shrilled as the First Sea Lord accompanied
Mr. Churchill over the side, and at least one observer
watched him descend with a prayer for the success of his
mission. The Admiral's barge moved gently on the swell at
the foot of the gangway, two statuesque sailors held her to
the ship with boat-hooks. The Prime Minister and the
Chiefs of Staff stepped aboard, Mr. Churchill gave a genial
wave of the hand to the faces gazing down at him from the

rail, and the barge sped across the intervening strip of water to the President's cruiser.

We watched Mr. Churchill mount the gangway of the *Augusta*; as his foot touched her deck, we heard a band play *God Save the King*, and we saw him standing at the salute. He then disappeared, to be seen a few moments later under the President's awning. Through glasses I could see him clearly—a broad, stocky figure in his blue suit, facing the President, who stood with his back to us against the guardrail. Mr. Churchill brought from his pocket a letter from the King, which he handed to the President with a slight bow. All this was still and formal, then suddenly the group moved and there were smiles and handshakes. Soon Mr. Churchill had brought out his cigar case and was smoking a cigar while the President lit a cigarette. In a few moments President and Prime Minister moved away from the awning out of view, followed by the British and American officers.

So the great secret which Brendan Bracken had introduced so mysteriously on a Saturday morning in London only a week ago had come to pass. The President had caught a fine fish, and Mr. Churchill was assisting at an interesting operation! Looking at the scene, the anchored ships, the melancholy hills, the grey sky, I thought how singular it was to be occupying a front seat at one of history's rare appearances, I say rare, because it is never easy for an observer of contemporary happenings to be absolutely certain that he is watching History or one of History's understudies, known as an event. "History in the making," Brendan Bracken had called it, and perhaps it was, but of that the future was the only judge. It had that touch of drama and romance that enliven a history book: the secret rendezvous, the guessing world, the swift voyage across seas open to the enemy; and I leaned on the guard rail, and, looking at the placid hills and the assembled ships, wondered if in years to come children will be taught the date—"Council of Placentia, August the ninth, 1941."

It is not difficult to find in history examples of famous journeys and meetings which have had a profound influence upon the world's destiny. Alexander the Great journeyed to Siwa to meet the God Ammon, one of history's remarkable encounters; after Caesar's murder, Antony, Octavian and Lepidus met to divide the world on an island in the river Lavinius; Cleopatra sailed to Tarsus to ally herself with Antony; Charlemagne journeyed to Rome to be crowned Emperor of the West; Henry VIII made a; picturesque, journey to France to meet Francis at the Field of the Cloth of Gold, and, in recent times, Napoleon met the Czar Alexander on a raft on the river Niemen. Yet there was no parallel in history that I could remember to the meeting at Placentia. Conquerors or would-be conquerors have met with only one object: to acquire new territories and greater dominion over Mankind, and, divested of their splendour and reduced to the lowest common denominator, such conferences might be compared with meetings between burglars who meet only to divide the swag. Here, at Placentia, something different was happening: the leaders of the two English-speaking nations were striving not for new territory or dominion over Mankind, but to prevent the carving up of the world and the enslavement of Humanity. Thus, I thought, it would indeed be strange if this Council of Placentia was not fated to be written in the pages of history, and if the date of August the ninth was not one which children still unborn may be required to know together with the dates of Magna Carta and the Declaration of Independence, and other such landmarks along the flinty road of Freedom.

In the course of the morning I learned some details of our programme. After the opening conference, which was then in progress, Mr. Churchill was returning to the *Prince of Wales*. There were staff meetings in the afternoon, and in the evening Mr. Churchill was to dine with President Roosevelt in the *Augusta*.

On the following day, Sunday, August 10th, there was to be an Anglo-American church parade service in the *Prince of Wales*. It was an idea that Mr. Churchill had been turning over in his mind on the way across, and the President had gladly agreed to it and had promised to attend. After the service Mr. Roosevelt was to be entertained to luncheon by Mr. Churchill. In the evening there were to be more staff talks and Mr. Churchill was again dining aboard the *Augusta*.

On Monday, August, 11th, the day was to be spent in further discussion between the two staffs and in private conversations between the President and the Prime Minister. On Tuesday, the twelfth, the discussions were to be concluded, and we were to leave Placentia Bay at five o'clock in the afternoon for home, breaking our journey at Iceland, where Mr. Churchill wished to inspect the Anglo-American garrison.

The afternoon of Saturday was enlivened by President Roosevelt's generosity to the ship's company. We saw approaching in motor boats, a pyramid of something like one thousand five hundred cardboard cartons, which a chain of American sailors had soon stacked on our quarter-deck.

Each carton contained an orange, two apples, two hundred cigarettes, and half a pound of cheese. There was a box for every sailor in the *Prince of Wales*, and inside each one was a card with the words: "The President of the United States of America sends his compliments and best wishes." It was a kindly thought which was enormously appreciated by our men.

While the pyramid was being distributed, Mr. Churchill came on deck and began to walk up and down alone smoking his cigar and thinking, no doubt, of the morning's meeting with the President. Official photographers were rather nervously manœuvring for pictures of the Americans and their gifts, wondering maybe if the Premier might object to such scenes upon the quarterdeck. But Mr. Churchill rarely objects to photographers. He walked up and was soon in sole charge of the operation.

"Come over here!" he called to the American sailors and then he grouped them with a number of British sailors. Stepping back, he critically examined the group.

"How's that?" he asked the photographers.

"Much better, sir," they replied.

"Wait a moment, don't take it yet!" said Mr. Churchill.

Waving his cigar at the sailors, he shouted, "More tooth!" The men immediately burst out laughing and the shutters clicked.

"A great guy," was the comment of one American seaman when Mr. Churchill, twinkling mischievously, took his place among them and was photographed. I reflected that in England we never think of Mr. Churchill as half American, as, of course, he is. How much of his energy and instinct for such practical affairs as restoring armoured trains to the

track under fire, the posing of press photographs and the
building of brick walls, comes from the Churchill side and
how much from the Jeromes of Rochester, N.Y., is an attrac-
tive speculation.

He is the child of a union between a duke's son and a
dollar princess, a romance that takes the mind in a nostalgic
flight to the last splendours of the nineteenth century in
England. His father, Lord Randolph Churchill, at the age of
twenty-four first saw Miss Jeannette Jerome, of Paris and
New York, aged nineteen, at a dance in a British cruiser
during Cowes Week in 1873; and with a decisive impetuos-
ity more familiar to us in his son, decided to marry her.
Winston Churchill has described the romance in one of the
best books a son has ever written about a father, his life of
Lord Randolph Churchill.

"That night—the third of their acquaintance," he wrote,
"was a beautiful night, warm and still, with the lights of the
yachts shining on the water and the sky bright with stars.
After dinner they found themselves alone together in the
garden and—brief courtship notwithstanding—he proposed and was accepted." Sixteen months later, the child of
the marriage, as if anxious to lose no time, was prematurely
born in Blenheim Palace.

Now, in a world changed out of all recognition, with
sixty-eight years separating a British cruiser in Cowes
Roads from an American cruiser off Newfoundland, the
son of that marriage, himself an Anglo-American alliance,
was trying to bring his two countries closer together in a
moment of world history. It would be generally alarming,
but altogether interesting, if fate granted to young lovers
one prescient glimpse into the future of their unborn child,

and I wonder what the young Randolph Churchill and the still more youthful Jeannette Jerome would have said on that warm night of stars could they have seen a well-nourished figure in a blue uniform saluting the President of the United States upon the ninth of August, in the year 1941, and have known that he was their Winston-to-be, Prime Minister and England's leader in her hour of peril. From what one has read of Lord Randolph's philosophic attitude towards the son who failed at first to pass into Sandhurst, it is perhaps likely that he would have questioned the accuracy of the oracle!

Resuming his walk, Mr. Churchill fell in with Spring and myself, and so we passed up and down the quarterdeck talking of many things until a staff officer came to take Mr. Churchill away. Spring happened to say that, so far, the voyage had been pleasant and delightful. Mr. Churchill, bestowing upon us a wicked wink, said (not altogether without relish!):

"We ain't home yet!"

He knew, but we did not know at the time, of the great wireless buzz then in progress, beginning, I think, at Cincinnati and spreading to Berne, and so over the Continent. The great secret had been well and truly exploded.

The assembled crews now began to indulge in an orgy of hospitality. British officers went visiting American ships and the Americans came to ours. Parties of American sailors came to the *Prince of Wales* and were entertained by our men and shown over the ship, while parties of our men were freely circulating between the *Augusta*, the *Tuscaloosa*, the *Arkansas* and the escorting destroyers.

Our ward-room was enriched by a strong flood of American literature. Fat magazines, such as *Esquire, Fortune, Life, The Saturday Evening Post, The American*, and many others, each one crammed with almost eatable coloured illustrations of gigantic boiled hams, roast beef and other rationed food, to say nothing of rich, creamy puddings, were piled high before our fascinated eyes.

Our American friends had evidently read something about a cigarette shortage in England, for they showered Lucky Strikes and Chesterfields upon us in almost embarrassing quantities. We, too, had something to dispense. As the American Navy is teetotal and its drinks are coca-cola, pineapple juice and iced coffee, the American officers showed no reluctance to assemble round the ward-room bar. And we, on that great occasion, were willing to discard the habits of a lifetime and to disregard the custom of the ship and open the bar at all kinds of peculiar times in order to return the generosity that was being recklessly expended upon us.

I soon became aware of a subtle and peculiar thing. Between ourselves and those charming and virile young Americans was the War, strange and impalpable as a curtain. It was not that they were not war-minded or sympathetic: it was simply that they were out of the War and knew nothing of it and could not imagine what it was really like. We must have been much the same at Munich. They belonged to peace-time still, to the prosperous, easy world of the fat ham advertisements in the magazines, a world of gleaming touring cars, new clothes, luxury, a world where money still meant almost everything. We were living in different time cycles; and I wondered if they were conscious of it, too.

After dinner in the *Augusta*. (L. to R.) Sir Alexander Cadogan, Sir Wilfrid Freeman, Mr. Churchill, President Roosevelt, Admiral Sir Dudley Pound, Sir John Dill, Lord Cherwell

"Goodbye and—safe voyage." the President and Mr. Churchill part on
the deck of the *Augusta,* August 12th, 1941

I realised, having perceived this, how much we must have changed at home in England unknown even to ourselves. In two years of war we have abandoned so much that is still of great importance to some people. It occurred to me that if some of the distinguished Englishmen who since the war have found themselves unable to leave the States should find it possible to return, what a shock would await them; for the England they remember no longer exists.

Mr. Churchill left in the admiral's barge that evening as he went off to dine with Mr. Roosevelt. I watched him go and then went in to dinner. When I came on deck again it was dark, and as I glanced around I caught my breath in amazement, for the ships were not blacked-out! They lay at anchor, rows of golden pin-points most beautiful to see, and beneath each ship the rows of lights wavered and trembled on the water. I had seen nothing like that for two years.

On shore, too, a dwelling invisible by day, perhaps a little shack or cabin, proclaimed itself by a spark that was a lighted window. How can I describe the heart-catching beauty of that sight? All Europe was dark, yet here in this lonely land, among deserted bays and barren hills, the lights were still shining, women had never caught up their infants to their breasts in fear, men had never crouched like animals in the dark listening to the sound of an enemy above them in the sky.

Most surprising of all was our own great ship, undarkened now for the first time in her life. She was the largest ship in the bay and she lay there like a memory of Brighton Pier. An officer told me that the American warships had made no black-out precautions, therefore it was decided to undarken the *Prince of Wales* because the presence among so many lights of one large dark battleship would have looked suspicious from the air.

"It's not likely that the Germans will send over long-range bombers," said this officer, "because they could never make the homeward journey. Still, you never know . . ."

I stayed there a long time, unable to leave that fearless scene.

X

CHURCH PARADE

THE sky cleared and the sun came out on Sunday, August 10th, for the first time in the course of our voyage. As in all bleak lands, it seemed as though a warm, transforming smile had spread over hills and sea, bringing out rich colours that had not been there before.

I met Mr. Churchill walking the deck, admiring the sun-lit beaches and the distant woods of fir and larch that rose up pin-sharp in the morning sun.

"We have a grand day for a church parade," he said, "and I have chosen some grand hymns."

I asked which he had chosen. He smiled.

"You'll hear," he said mysteriously.

Sailors were already arranging the quarter-deck for the church parade. Upon the starboard side they placed two chairs, one for the President, the other for the Prime Minister, slightly in advance of others for the British and American Chiefs of Staff. In the centre of the quarter-deck, facing the four guns of the fourteen-inch turret, was a lectern draped with the Union Jack and the Stars and Stripes. Mr. Churchill walked about inspecting every detail, often taking a hand by moving a chair an inch one way or another and by pulling out the folds of the Union Jack.

In a short while there converged upon our ship from all parts of Placentia Bay boatloads of American sailors standing tightly packed, their white rimless caps shining in the morning light. As they came aboard, they were greeted by our lads and then they streamed together in groups to the quarter-deck, for on the Prime Minister's instructions there was to be no marching about but complete informality. The men were told to mix together as they liked, British and American, and to line both sides of the quarter-deck, and also the space amidships under the guns. The band of the Royal Marines was posted under the gun turret facing the lectern,

The American destroyer *McDougal*, which had been secured alongside the *Augusta*, cast off and came slowly steaming round our bows with the President and his staff upon her bridge. She edged up inch by inch to us and her deck was level with ours. She secured to us and a gangway was thrown across. Mr. Churchill and the three Chiefs of Staff stood at our end of the gangway beside a guard of honour and a band of Royal Marines.

We saw the President come forward, leaning on the arm of a young American Air Corps officer—his son, Captain Elliott Roosevelt. It is well known that since August, 1921, President Roosevelt has fought an heroic and ceaseless battle against infantile paralysis. In that year he left New York, where that terrible disease was raging, for a holiday in Maine. Having put out a fire in the Maine Woods, he swam in ice-cold water, and was afterwards seized by a deathly chill which developed into infantile paralysis. Many a man would have become a helpless invalid, but Franklin D. Roosevelt decided to fight his opponent every inch of the way. The splendour of that effort shines in his calm, carved face, the face of a St. George who has trampled the dragon under him. While we gazed at him in admiration, he stepped slowly forward, tall and erect, leaning upon the arm of his son, and, as his foot touched our deck, the band played *The Star Spangled Banner* and the guard presented arms. President Roosevelt stood there, his head bared, wearing a blue lounge suit. On the gangway behind him stood the Chiefs of the American fighting services: Admiral Harold Stark, Chief of Naval Operations; Admiral King, C.-in-C. of the American Battle Fleet; General George Marshall, Chief of Staff of the U.S. Army; General Arnold, of the Air Force; Brigadier-General George Watson, Military Secretary to the President. Among the naval, military and air force uniforms were some civilian clothes: Mr. Sumner Welles, Under-Secretary of State, Mr. Averell Harriman and Mr. Harry Hopkins.

As soon as the anthem had ended, Mr. Churchill stepped forward and shook hands with the President, and side by side they walked to the chairs on the quarterdeck. As soon as they were seated with the Chiefs of Staff behind them, the service began. The British Chaplain and the American Chaplain stood together facing the lectern, and advanced in turn to read the prayers. This prayer was offered for the President of the United States:

O Lord, High and Mighty, Ruler of the Universe, look with favour we beseech thee, Upon the President of the United States of America, and all others in authority. Grant them in health and prosperity long to live. We ask this in the Name of Him who liveth and reigneth world without end.—Amen.

The British Chaplain offered a prayer for King George VI, which was followed by a prayer for the oppressed countries:

> Let us pray for the invaded countries in the grief and havoc of oppression; for the upholding of their courage; and the hope for the speedy restoration of their freedom. O Lord God, whose compassions fail not, support, we entreat thee, the peoples on whom the terrors of invasion have fallen: and if their liberty be lost to the oppressor, let not this spirit and hope be broken, but stayed upon thy strength till the day of deliverance. Through Jesus Christ, our Lord.

Then the first of the hymns chosen by Mr. Churthill went roaring out over the silent bay:

O God our help in ages past ...

The British and Americans stood together in close ranks, their caps off, their heads bent over the hymn sheets. It was difficult now that the little white caps had been doffed to say who was American and who was British; and the sound of their voices rising together in the hymn was carried far out over the sea. In the long, frightful panorama of this War, a panorama full of guns and tanks crushing the life out of men, of women and children weeping and of homes blasted into rubble by bombs, there had been no scene like this, a scene, it seemed, from another world, conceived on lines different from anything known to the pageant-masters of the Axis, a scene rooted in the first principles of European civilisation which go back to the figure of Charlemagne kneeling before the Pope on Christmas morning.

The service continued. Captain Leach read the Lessons, and the second of Mr. Churchill's hymns was announced—"*Onward, Christian Soldiers.*" The deep voices rose again through the still morning and the other ships far out in the bay must have heard it clearly and have recognised it as they sang.

> At the sign of triumph
> Satan's host doth flee;
> On then Christian soldiers,
> On to Victory.

I watched the two men in the seats of honour, the tall man and the smaller man in blue, who together represented the people of Britain and the United States; and I wondered what was passing through their minds at that moment. Churchill was affected emotionally, as I knew he would be. His handkerchief stole from its pocket. What was he seeing, I wondered, for his mind embraces wide vistas, as he looked round the decks of that warship where the fingers of the wind were gently bringing together the folds of the Union Jack and the Stars and Stripes, where British sailors and Americans stood shoulder to shoulder, so alike most of them that they might have been brothers. Perhaps he will tell us some day what was passing in his mind that Sunday morning; and perhaps the tall man with the calm, carved features will tell us, too.

There came a prayer for the victory of Right and Truth:

Save us and deliver us from the hands of our enemies; abate their pride, assuage their malice, and confound their devices;

that we, being armed with thy defence, may be preserved ever more from all perils, to glorify Thee, who art the only giver of all victory.

Stablish our hearts, O God, in the day of battle, and strengthen our resolve, that we fight not in enmity against men but against the powers of darkness enslaving the souls of men, till all the enmity and oppression be done away and the peoples of the world be set free from fear to serve one another as children of our Father, who is above all and through all and in all, our God for ever and ever.

The voices were lifted in a majestic hymn, the choice, not of Mr. Churchill, but of President Roosevelt. When the Prime Minister, on the preceding day, hymn-book in hand had consulted the President in his cabin aboard the *Augusta* on the order of the service, Mr. Roosevelt had said, "But you must have '*Eternal Father, strong to save*'." Now, as the voices rose and fell, a situation that was almost intolerable in its uncalculated emotionalism reached breaking-point. I have seen many poignant, heart-searching ceremonies in my time. I saw the Victory March through London at the end of the last War. I was present in St. Paul's when King George V and Queen Mary returned thanks for victory. I was in Westminster Abbey when the Unknown Soldier was buried. I saw the Menin Gate unveiled upon the blasted ramparts of Ypres. I saw George V carried to his grave. I was in the House of Commons when a king gave up his crown, and in Westminster Abbey when another king was anointed.

All these events pulled at the heart in their different ways, and the scene upon the quarter-deck of a British battleship in war-time, yet so far from the War, was of that order, too. We from England had come to it fresh from two bitter years of struggle, years in which some of our best friends thought our time had come. But it had not, and we held on alone; and war can be very lonely at times. The scene before us upon our battleship that morning was certainly a symbol of unity, might it not also have been a promise of alliance? As the sound of the last hymn died away, those lines by Arthur Hugh Clough, which Churchill sent to Roosevelt by the hand of Wendell Willkie, came to my mind:

> And not by eastern windows only,
> When daylight comes, comes in the light,
> In front, the sun climbs slow, how slowly,
> But Westward, look, the land is bright.

I wonder whether Mr. Churchill was thinking of that, too.

Slowly and solemnly over the hushed gathering came like a benediction those exquisite words that are ordered to be said every day in the Royal Navy:

O Eternal Lord God, Who alone spreadest out the heavens, and rulest the raging of the sea; Who hast compassed the waters with bounds until day and night come to an end; Be pleased to receive into Thy Almighty and Most Gracious protection the persons of us Thy servants, and the Fleet in which we serve. Preserve us from the dangers of the sea, and from the violence of the enemy; that we may be a security for such as pass upon the seas upon their lawful occasions; that the peoples of the Empire may in peace and quietness serve Thee,

our God; and that we may return in safety to enjoy the bless-
ings of the land, with the fruits of our labours, and with a
thankful remembrance of Thy mercies to praise and glorify
Thy Holy Name; through Jesus Christ our Lord.

The service was over.

Thank God for men with cameras and sailors who secrete
kodaks in their blouses, for, with a splendid rush, we
descended from the peaks of feeling into regions where it
was easier to breathe with dignity and control. No sooner
had the parade been concluded than an extraordinary scene
occurred. British and American sailors, first timidly, then
like the toughest of Press cameramen, began to creep and
crawl towards the President and the Prime Minister.
Outraged officers were prepared to order them away, but the
President and the Prime Minister smiled and encouraged
them; so there was nothing to be done about it.

The sacred quarter-deck of a British battleship has probably never witnessed such a scene. Sailors crawled like snakes
to within a yard of the great men and snapped their kodaks
in their faces. And Mr. Roosevelt, smoking a cigarette and
Mr. Churchill smoking a cigar, nodded and smiled, and
waved their hands, as if they were at home indulging the
photographic ambitions of a band of zealous and agile neph-
ews. What amused me considerably was that certain officers,
who had been only too willing to stop this disgraceful exhi-
bition, ran helter-skelter to their cabins and, returning with
cameras, joined in!

Both victims were superb. They sat there smiling at each
other and chatting until every spool of film had been

expended, then, of course, the situation solved itself. The photographers melted away, glowing with the pride of achievement, and the President and the Prime Minister were at last alone.

Mr. Roosevelt and his Chiefs of Staff were entertained to luncheon by Mr. Churchill in the ward-room of the *Prince of Wales*. Great preparations had been made. Before he left London, Mr. Churchill, wondering what he could take that would be unusual, seasonable and definitely British, decided to take grouse. As grouse shooting had opened on August 1st, it was arranged that sufficient birds for the luncheon party, and an extra brace for the President, should be put on the train at Perth. It is typical of the Prime Minister that he should have remembered it was once the custom of the Lords of Admiralty when they voyaged abroad to take with them a turtle, which they were entitled to draw from a naval establishment. This strange custom began when Britain, in order to watch Napoleon at St. Helena, took over Ascension Island, and every warship on its way to England from Ascension Island brought a turtle home with it. The custom has, of course, long since lapsed and Mr. Churchill, even if he would have revived it, might have been hard put to it to discover a turtle in wartime London. Nevertheless he managed to serve turtle soup to the President. It so happened that shortly before the party left London, Commander Thompson, who had heard Mr. Churchill wish for a turtle, was in a grocer's shop in Piccadilly and, noticing some bottles of turtle soup and finding that neither coupons nor ration books were required for them, promptly bought them and took them back in triumph to No. 10.

There were two speeches at the luncheon tables—one by Mr. Churchill, the other by the President. Afterwards Mr. Roosevelt entered the ante-room and, sitting with Mr. Churchill, shook hands with the ships' officers as they filed past. The afternoon was well advanced when the President's destroyer made ready to cast off. Mr. Churchill accompanied his guest to the gangway and shook him warmly by the hand as he crossed to his own ship. During the preparations for departure, just before the gangway was lifted, a small dignified person who had not been seen on deck before, appeared with, the air of a contemptuous admiral and began to follow the President aboard his destroyer. It was Blackie, the senior cat of the *Prince of Wales*. As his intention to leave the ship and claim American nationality was obvious, the grin that broke out on the faces of sailors was communicated to the faces of the American sailors in the Presidential destroyer. But no one could do anything because everyone was standing to attention. Mr. Churchill saved Blackie for England by bending down and leading him from the gangway.

As the destroyer steamed, away from us, Mr. Churchill stood alone at the guard-rail waving to the President, then he turned to pace up and down the quarter-deck.

An officer, bursting with enthusiasm, told me that when the President had departed, he with some others approached Mr. Churchill and thanked him for the honour of having been invited to luncheon.

"It's an honour for us all," said Mr. Churchill. "And great things may come of it in the future. You have seen a great man this day."

He turned away, but came back and spoke to the officers.

"On this lovely day," he said, "the sun shining as it is on this beautiful harbour, surrounded as we are by American men of war, it is difficult for you and me to realise that we are fighting for our very lives."

His manner became grim and he snapped out the last words in a ringing voice, as if he were addressing a public meeting.

"And, do you know," commented the officer who told me of this, "I really believe old Winston would die fighting in the streets, if it came to that!"

After his daily hour in bed, the weather still lovely, Mr. Churchill decided he would spend a little time ashore. A whaler was brought round to the gangway towed by a motor launch. Mr. Churchill appeared on deck dressed again in his siren suit in company with Mr. Averell Harriman, Sir Alexander Cadogan, Commander Thompson and Mr. Martin. We watched them depart and an hour or so later we saw them returning. Mr. Churchill was sitting in the whaler holding a bunch of pink wild flowers he had collected on the beaches and the hills.

In the evening the Prime Minister dined with the President. Just as he was leaving he asked me if I did not think the church parade had been a wonderful and moving sight. As if talking to himself, he said. "The same language, the same hymns and, more or less, the same ideals . . . ." Then in the same tone of voice, he added. "I have an idea that something really big may he happening—something really big. . . ."

He turned away and descended the gangway to the launch.

That night the ships were lit only until ten o'clock. At that time the first black-out was made in the American ships, and with it a European darkness descended upon Placentia Bay.

XI

WE GO ASHORE

I HEARD that Monday, August 11th, was to be a day of almost continuous conferences aboard the President's cruiser. As Spring and I were not able to visit that ship, there was nothing for us to do but watch the arrival and departure of ships' launches, an occupation that, after a time, lost its charm.

The desire to go ashore and see what Newfoundland was like was so hard to bear that I decided to try and get permission to do so.

The rule that no one was to leave the ship in order to prevent any leakage of information was, of course, a wise and proper regulation, for who could say what enterprising persons might have flown from the States, or Canada, to Newfoundland? However, I decided to appeal to Mr. Churchill and, to my delight, he gained permission for Spring and myself to accompany Paymaster-Commander Wheeler, who with a mess steward was going ashore that morning on the ship's business.

With the excitement of a couple of schoolboys who had been given an unexpected holiday, Spring and I stepped into a speed cutter with "Pay" and the steward. The weather had turned again. Rain was falling and the bay was tipped with white. The cutter set off with a tremendous roar and, skimming over the water, received upon its flat hull the powerful blows of each advancing wave, sending back over the little cabin in which we sat showers of salt spray. I was thrilled and happy. Not to have set foot on Newfoundland would have irked and worried me at moments for the rest of my life. I think one of the hardest trials of a sailor's existence must be to see, but never to land in, strange countries; and that often happens in the Navy, especially in wartime.

Having raced through the water for about half an hour, we came within sight of the gaunt outline of a range of tall buildings in course of construction. The air was loud with the sound of hammering and the roar of lorry engines changing gear on bad roads. The tall steel frameworks were an extraordinary apparition, in so primitive a landscape, and the name of this place was Argentia, one of the leased American sea-plane bases. The buildings were rising on land that had never until then known anything except a humble cod-fishing and curing station, and we saw some of the fishing boats at anchor in a small creek.

We tied up to a wooden jetty. Above us, twirling a wooden baton, just like a "cop" in a film, stood an American military policeman. We explained ourselves and started to walk through clusters of wooden huts marooned in mud and approached by duck-boards. All around us were skeleton steel buildings and a network of unmade roads. The place was a pleasing confirmation of my idea of an Alaskan town during a gold boom. Tough-looking men wearing check shirts of irreconcilable colours strode about or came splashing through the mud in ancient Fords, their trousers, or "pants," held up by leather belts; and there was not a woman or child to be seen.

I had often seen Argentia on the films. I thought it was only a question of time before we met the sheriff, the "doc," and the local blonde, and only a matter maybe of minutes before someone fired a six-shooter. But I was wrong, as a few questions put to a passer-by proved beyond question. There were no bars or saloons, no blonde, no sheriffs, probably no six-shooters; and the men lived in messes and saved up their money because there was nothing to buy with it, or else they dutifully posted it home to their families. Imported American labour had been augmented by the local fishermen who had discovered that building was vastly more profitable than catching cod-fish. The primitive little wooden platform upon which the fishermen had for centuries cleaned and dried the fish and extracted cod-liver oil was standing there deserted, and in the anchored boats the fishers, turned labourers, lived and slept.

We found our way to the office of the camp contractor, where "Pay" explained that, as the crew of the *Prince of Wales* were not allowed ashore, he desired, if possible, to buy such stores as cheese, sugar, tea and tins of salmon which the men might buy and post home to their families when we reached England. The contractor said "sure." He said "sure" to 100 lbs. of tea and also 100 lbs. of cheese. He promised to find out about sugar and salmon and offered us a great quantity of chocolate. Highly gratified, we left the mess steward in charge and went off to a slightly apprehensive little wooden bank where we changed £250 into tight wads of Canadian dollars.

We then visited the recreation room, which was a remarkable building decorated with various kinds of varnished woods like marquetry. It was furnished with canvas

camp furniture and the windows were darkened by mos-
quito netting. While we waited there, "Pay," who had been
vaguely mysterious for some time, disappeared, and Spring
and I were left gazing through the darkened windows at the
gloomy scene outside where a thin drizzle was falling over
the muddy landscape and the gaunt camp. Spring saw some
irises flourishing in a swamp, and he thought they would
grow well in Cornwall. He went out into the rain and
grubbed up a number of bulbs, which he wrapped in newspaper. An American major emerged from his office and said
that a "very important journalist" who was flying from
London to Placentia had got lost, and everyone was worried
sick about him. We asked his name; but the major then
became mysterious. We felt it was hard to have emerged
from so much mystery only to encounter it again the
moment we touched land.

We wondered whether London had misunderstood our
predicament and had sent out some authentic hot newspaperman to do what we had failed to do, someone who
would break the boycott and shame us for ever, someone
who would fire off scoop after scoop while we sank shame-
fully into the background. So we grovelled in self-abasement
for some time until the same thought struck us at the same
moment, and we said: "It's the Beaver!"

"Pay" came back, still rather mysterious, to say that he
had been to meet the Governor of Newfoundland who was
in a railway siding not far off. He had arrived from St. John's
in a special train and was due to lunch with the Prime
Minister aboard the ship. "Pay" was much interested in the
train, which was a queer little two-coach train drawn by a
locomotive with a cow-puncher and a bell, the sort of train

you see at Hamleys. We asked if he knew that Lord Beaverbrook was on his way by air, and from the spasm of surprise which crossed his honest face, we knew that our guess was correct.

Having settled the question of supplies so easily, we thought we would be justified in taking a trip to the town of Placentia to have luncheon and to see what the place was like. I was delighted with this arrangement, for the one thing I wanted above everything else on earth was to buy a portable typewriter. My own machine had been demolished in a "blitz" and not one key had been left. I asked an American officer if I would be able to buy a typewriter in Placentia.

"I guess not," he replied, "but you can try." We hired a Ford four-seater and set off through the mud, bumping and ploughing over the atrocious roads. The base was an interesting phenomenon. It was bounded by a wire fence and everything inside the fence was American. The Stars and Stripes flew there. Cars kept to the right of the road. As soon as we passed outside the fence we were in a British possession and we changed over to the left of the road. But in practice the roads were so bad that, whether in the United States or Newfoundland one drove wherever there were fewer pot-holes.

The country was melancholy and not at all unlike the Hebrides or the Shetlands. Dwarf Christmas trees climbed the hills and clouds hung low over the land, irises sprang from bogs and brown streams gurgled through the peat. We passed no one but a man driving a cart, and once we had left the outskirts of Argentia there was never a cabin or a house to be seen. After travelling for five miles, we came to a swiftly flowing arm of the sea on whose further bank we saw the little town of Placentia standing white and clean. One glance told me that my search for a typewriter would be in vain.

There was no bridge across the water, therefore we had to leave the car to await our return and we walked down to the water's edge and whistled for the ferry. This was a coffin-like craft known, I believe, as a dory. Stepping ashore on the opposite bank, we set off to walk towards the small group of white wooden houses which formed the town of Placentia. Most of them were white-washed and they stood in an irregular, haphazard manner here and there, standing back behind white wooden fences in their bleak gardens. Another arm of the sea flowed through Placentia, a fine, deep stretch of water that looked like a perfect Scottish salmon river, peat-brown and so clear that you could see every stone and pebble in the bed. There were stones and pebbles everywhere in Placentia, and I noticed that the town is built on a shingle beach that juts out between two inlets from the bay.

The population is now about three thousand and the town is an ancient one. Its site was sold to the French by Charles II in 1660 and I believe it takes its name from an adjacent hill, which the French called Plaisance. One of the articles of the Treaty of Utrecht obliged the French to surrender all territory in Newfoundland and to evacuate Placentia, which they did in the year 1713.

We walked along the rutty road beside the water and then, turning inland, came to what was evidently the centre of the town, if such a delightfully haphazard group of dwellings can claim to have a centre. Here was the only large building, a huge Roman Catholic church made entirely of wood painted white, and with an imposing baroque tower

Mr. Churchill in Iceland saluting the American Colours

Mr. Churchill in Iceland with Ensign Franklin D. Roosevelt

at the north-western end. Next to it was the priests' house, the only stone building in the place. There was a 1914–1918 war memorial outside the west door on which I was interested to read some two hundred good Irish names such as Ryan, Callaghan and O'Reilly.

The shops in Placentia, on whose treasures we, like all ship-bound mariners, had been building fantastic hopes, were nothing more than wooden shacks or the bottom storeys of ordinary houses with nothing inside one could possibly require. There were not more than six or seven of them. Nearly everything in these shops came from the United States or Canada. There were plentiful supplies of American canned food and in Mr. Ryan's store we discovered several boxes of what appeared to us to be superb American silk stockings in cellophane envelopes at one dollar and a few cents a pair—just under five shillings. As not one of us fortunately could remember the size of his wife's feet, we were spared the embarrassing ordeal of buying them. "Pay," who was desperately anxious to justify his position as mess president, achieved a minor triumph in the purchase of twenty-four small apples.

Spring sat on a boulder in the main street and said that Placentia was the place he had been looking for all his life, and I agreed that a man could be almost perfectly happy there. There was no visible cinema, probably few wireless sets, no motor-cars, no newspapers and only a very rudimentary telephone system carried on sturdy tree trunks. There was also an almost total absence of townsfolk. And there was no black-out.

We were wondering where we could get luncheon when we encountered Huckleberry Finn. He was a tousled-headed

youth in torn pants and a floppy hat who was sitting on a
fence whittling a chip of wood with a pen-knife and hum-
ming under his breath. We asked where we could get
something to eat.

"You wanner turkey dinner?" he asked.

We thought it sounded ambitious but good, and allowed
him to lead us to a small white wooden house which stood
back behind a fenced garden. It bore upon its door the words
"Hospitality Café." When we stepped inside we saw that the
front parlour had been fitted up with five or six tables as a
little restaurant, and we might have been in Margate. The
only thing missing was an aspidistra in a draped flower-pot.
A perfect specimen of the what-not stood there loaded with
ornaments; and the pictures, mostly of angelic apparitions,
were of the kind seen only in English seaside lodgings. We
could not imagine by what process this little English room
had been transported to Newfoundland as if carried intact
by the wind across the Atlantic.

Having always understood that Newfoundland was not
Britain's most prosperous possession, our eyes jumped from
our heads when we read the menu, which contained "roast
chicken," "roast turkey," "beef steak," "grilled ham," to say
nothing of numerous cold dishes. Still wondering if this
could be true, we turned to greet a woman in glasses with a
head of the most lovely auburn hair.

"Howdy, folks!" she said.

We replied "Howdy," and asked how long beef steaks
would be. She said twenty minutes. Alas, it is another tragedy of a sailor's life that, while he is ashore there is hardly a
moment when he is not haunted by the memory of an
appointment with a launch or a small boat that is to return

him to his ship. One of the greatest crimes is to keep those horrible little boats waiting or to miss them altogether, for they are merciless little boats and their god is a clock or a wrist watch. Our appointment with one of those tyrants was not far off, therefore we could not wait twenty minutes even for a beef steak.

"Well," said the lady, "what say to three fried ham sandwiches, cheese, butter and special caw-fee?"

We said "fine," and in a few moments the smell of frying ham floated through the small house. The lady entered with a pound of golden butter, a huge cheese, and a tin of water-biscuits, which she called "crackers." She soon returned with three gigantic sandwiches, each one bulging with about half a pound of fried ham, and a percolator full of excellent coffee, and a bowl of whipped cream. We crouched over this meal like criminals while the lady stood near and talked to us.

We asked what the inhabitants of Placentia did for their living. She replied that she "wouldn't know" because she had been there only four and a half years. We suggested that she was just getting to know one or two people, and she "guessed" that was so. She put her hand up to her beautiful hair, and said wistfully that she had once lived in Noo York. "Pay," spreading a thick carpet of butter on a biscuit, said what a change it must be, to come from New York to Placentia. The lady said: "Oh boy—*and* how!"

I glanced round the little room, at the honest food on the table, at the windows which had never known black-out curtains, realising that Newfoundland, although technically at war, was still within the orbit of the peaceful States. Yet how astonishing it was to encounter in Newfoundland, and in a little backwater like Placentia, a meal that could not be served in the wartime Ritz.

It was unfortunate that we had to finish the feast in a hurry and almost run through Placentia to the ferry, on the further side of which our car was patiently waiting. When we arrived at Argentia, we found the mess steward in a state of depression. The contractor, who had been so "sure" of everything, had since checked up his stores and had discovered with regret that he was unable to spare anything. So we returned empty-handed to the ship, "Pay" carrying a little black bag full of tight wads of Canadian dollars.

I shall never forget Placentia, as one never forgets any place seen in such hurried and unusual circumstances. One day I shall go back there.

I have unearthed an odd piece of information about it. Placentia's one distinguished, or notorious, son was a prophet named Richard Brothers who made a great stir in London society during the reign of George III. He was born at Placentia in 1757, the son of an Irish immigrant. When a boy, Brothers was sent home to England, where he passed through Woolwich and entered the Royal Navy as a midshipman. He saw action under Keppel and Rodney, and was retired on half-pay as a lieutenant when he was twenty-six years of age. After some years abroad, he came to London when he was in the thirties, and began to show signs of peculiarity. He conceived the idea that he was the nephew of the Deity, and had a divine mission to perform. He issued a number of prophecies, some of which came true, and so he gathered about him the usual band of credulous people who always follow a plausible lunatic. Among his followers was a Member of Parliament, the oriental scholar, N. B. Halhed, M.P. for Lymington.

Brothers had a genius for getting himself mixed up in politics, which was not to be wondered at because the first essential to his mission was the dethronement of George III. Having assumed the English crown, Brothers then intended to lead his followers, and all the Jews, back to Palestine where they would found the New Jerusalem. The prophet was such an insistent publicist and letter-writer that the Government had to take action, with the result that Brothers spent a long time confined in mad-houses and other similar institutions.

Like all fanatics, he had a highly developed gift of persuasion, and his followers never questioned him when he ordered them to sell their earthly goods and prepare to follow him to the New Jerusalem in the year 1795. When nothing happened, his reputation was slightly shaken, but he continued to pour out a stream of prophecy for another twenty years, when eventually he died in great poverty. As a mad Messiah, there was nothing unusual about Brothers. He was only one of several similar fanatics at that time. There was Ann Lee of Manchester, who became a "shaker" and went to America; there was Johanna Southcott, and, strangest of all, Mother Buchan, the Scottish seer. This crazy woman persuaded her followers to fast for forty days and shave the top of their heads, leaving only a top-knot to serve as a handle for the angels who, upon a certain day, would draw them up to heaven. When the emaciated gathering assembled on a hill top expecting to be transported, and nothing happened, Mother Buchan's fortunes, like those of Brothers', suffered a decline, but there were always some who still believed. One of these, after her death, preserved her mummified corpse for fifty years, annually expecting its resurrection. Beside these strange mental freaks, the prophet of Placentia is almost an ordinary bore. He lies buried in St. John's Wood, appropriately enough on the opposite side of the cemetery to Johanna Southcott.

When we returned to the ship, we found a large number of American officers assembled there. We learned that there was to be a guest night. When dinner-time arrived, about eighty British and American officers sat down at the long tables, which, cleared of their cloths, were seen to be of polished mahogany. Candles were lighted in sconces and, as the guests took their seats, the band of the Royal Marines played them in to dinner.

The mess president had managed to find enough red and white wine to go round, and the cooks had excelled themselves with the rations. By the way, the officers in the *Prince of Wales* drew exactly the same rations as the men. The port held out valiantly, and went round four times. At its first passing, the Commander stood and proposed the health of the President, and we stood while the band played *The Star Spangled Banner.* The senior American officer then proposed "The King," and the band played the Anthem. Cigarette smoke began to curl round the candles.

It has always been the custom in the Royal Navy that when the formality of a guest night begins to melt in port, the younger members of a ward-room scent a "rag." I waited, wondering what would happen. There was not long to wait. Without warning came a number of shattering explosions, accompanied by a smell of explosives, and, for a moment perhaps, some of our guests may have thought that we had been torpedoed, for they looked round anxiously and eventually detected two young lieutenants who had flung thunder-flashes under the table. The band plunged into a merry tune, and the port went round again.

A young American officer, expanding in the genial atmosphere, said to his neighbour: "I guess you boys take this War very lightly."

The man he had addressed had told me in conversation that he had been torpedoed in the *Royal Oak*, and that his home in Plymouth had been bombed and not a thing saved.

"Oh rather," he replied, with a hearty laugh, "why not?"

And I thought what a confoundedly deceptive race we are.

We moved from the dining-room to the ante-room, where you could positively sense events to come. I reflected that this was to be undoubtedly the first "rag" ever held in the *Prince of Wales*, and I thought how interesting it was to see the younger members of the party slip back so easily into a peace-time guest night. And how richly those boys had earned that brief respite from war. I had seen them on the way across at their action stations at all hours of the day and night. I had heard them describe a battle at sea, and I had detected the grey war look in the eyes of the most juvenile. I sat back with pleasure awaiting the outburst of animal spirits. George Ferguson, like a wicked blue elf, was ominously flitting about in the background among his juniors.

Suddenly there arose a wild and horrible skirl of pipes, and into the ward-room marched a charming lad named Forbes, kilted, with the pipes over his arm, and accompanied by a grotesque companion, also kilted, and furnished with a set of bright pink whiskers. They marched round so solemnly, threatening at the same time to lift the girders of the ward-room with their horrible lament, that some of our guests, unfamiliar perhaps with our more exotic moments, wondered if this might not be some fine old Scottish custom, and politely refrained from laughter. But the pipers suddenly quickened the tune and marched straight over arm-chairs and settees as if they were surmounting their native obstacles; and then everyone roared with laughter and the Americans flung themselves into the "rag" with abandon.

Their talent lay chiefly in music. The ward-room piano, a patient instrument, was dragged out and one after the other, guests occupied the chair to rounds of applause. It was a good scene and it went on for a long time, so long indeed that I found myself unable to keep awake and went down to my cabin, wondering how it was going to end.

I heard in the morning that the damage to furniture was not excessive considering all things. I was told that when a young Marine officer was stripped to the waist and carried on a stretcher by picked teams of British and American youth over a difficult steeplechase course composed of the ward-room furniture, the evening had touched its zenith, and from then onwards began to wilt and decline. Everyone agreed that everyone else was a dashed good fellow; so what could have been finer?

In the still small hours, at five o'clock to be precise, an energetic man with a much-cartooned smile came across Placentia Bay in one of the ship's launches. He had taken off from England in an aircraft which had crossed safely to

St. John's but was unable to get to Placentia Bay. The passenger made himself known with accustomed vigour and hired a special train. The train had taken him to Placentia; and now—at last—Lord Beaverbrook came aboard the *Prince of Wales.*

XII

THE ATLANTIC CHARTER

A DAY of almost continuous conferences, the passing to and
fro of launches, Mr. Churchill and Lord Beaverbrook striding about the deck like a couple of pirate kings, then
descending the gangway and setting off to see the President—
that was Tuesday, August 12th.

Lord Beaverbrook was in great spirits, and his journey
out seemed to have stimulated him. The special train in
which he had crossed the peninsula was kept waiting at
Argentia, and I heard that when we had sailed that evening
he was returning to St. John's in it, and was then flying to
Washington to continue the discussions.

As afternoon approached, there were many signs of our
impending departure. The ship's launches were gradually
called in and hoisted aboard. The crew became busy at a
hundred tasks, preparing the ship for sea. Captain Leach disappeared again. American officers rushed up to the
ward-room to say good-bye and to press a final copy of *Life*
or *Esquire*, or a cheese, into the hands of their friends in the
Prince of Wales.

Meanwhile in the *Augusta* the President and Mr. Churchill
were concluding their conversation. Launches were in per-
petual motion between the *Prince of Wales* and the President's

Cruiser; secretaries and others ran up the gangways, disappeared and returned with papers and documents. The great men ended their discussions with a pleasing little ceremony. Mr. Churchill had brought with him from England several illuminated copies of the Longfellow Verse, "O Ship of State" which Mr. Roosevelt had sent written in his own hand by Mr. Wendell Willkie in the dark days of the Blitz. These copies were signed by both men, the President kept one and Mr. Churchill another. Then the President and the Prime Minister exchanged autographed portraits.

At length, as the afternoon advanced, the last launch steamed from the *Augusta*, the Prime Minister and the Chiefs of Staff were aboard, and at four forty-five Lord Beaverbrook said good-bye and departed in a motor boat. The gangway came in the anchors came up. The battleship began to vibrate. On the stroke of five she turned and passed slowly from the bay, saluting the *Augusta* as she did so. The clock was immediately advanced two hours. We had just had tea. It was at once seven o'clock and dinner-time.

We were escorted by the destroyers *Reading*, *Ripley*, *Assiniboine* and *Saguenay*. Two American destroyers also sailed in company but did not form part of our screen, the *Mayrant* and *Rhind*. When we came to the open sea those two ships steamed off and took station four miles ahead. They were going to Iceland with Ensign Franklin Roosevelt who had been attached as A.D.C. to Mr. Churchill by the President during the Premier's tour of the island.

Surgeon-Commander Quinn was called to see the Prime Minister, who had slightly strained a leg muscle during one of his many passages up and down gangways and ladders. The doctor prescribed rest and massage by one of the medical staff.

I viewed our return voyage with some trepidation. I detested the thought of spending six more nights in Cabin 27. I also wondered, how my nerves would stand up to a naval action, for everyone was now anticipating with some pleasure a battle on the way home; at least, everyone except myself. Some thought U-boats would lie in wait for us; others thought long-range bombers; a few enthusiasts thought U-boats and long-range bombers, and I was inclined to throw in the *Tirpitz* and a few cruisers as well.

I knew that the time had now come to take my Mae West seriously. I had not worn it on the way out, although I had taken the precaution to remove it from its shelf every night and place it near the bunk. While I was changing for dinner that night, I discovered that by putting on the life-belt beneath my waistcoat, the slight abdominal swelling was hardly noticeable, indeed the only indication that I was wearing my Mae West was a faint smell of rubber and a band visible only to myself that looked like the top of a dirty cummerbund. For a few moments I practised "abandon ship" in the solitude of my cabin, flinging off my dinner jacket and inflating the Mae West until I was encircled by a warm and consoling tyre. I let out the air again with the conviction that, should the worst happen, I might be able to go through these motions in the dark and on a windy deck. Feeling unusually buoyant, I went up to dinner.

We learned that Mr. Churchill's cinema was to be resumed that night. Unfortunately, there was considerable delay, and, as we hung about waiting for the show to begin, it became evident that while we had put on the clock, Mr. Churchill had not. It was eleven o'clock—but only nine o'clock to him—when the film began. It was Paulette Goddard in *Ghost Breakers.*

It was a long way past midnight when the film ended, and we were a weary audience. The Chiefs of Staffs looked exhausted, too, but not the Prime Minister, who was just perking up and becoming more lively than ever, pink and cherubic, and apparently utterly unaffected by the exertions of the past days. Outstanding ability, or genius, if you like, may have something to do, as Carlyle believed, with a transcendent capacity for taking trouble, but I have an idea that unusual physical ability explains quite a lot.

Those of us who were not already awake at half-past seven the following morning, Wednesday, August 13th, were roused by the voice of the Captain magnified by loud-speakers all over the ship.

He told us that the meeting between the Prime Minister and the President had certainly become known in Germany, and that probably it was known also that the meeting had taken place off Newfoundland. He said that the danger of submarine attack was imminent and as we approached home, the danger of air attack must not be overlooked. He therefore called upon all members of the ship's company, especially those concerned with gun stations, submarine detection, and damage repairs to be "on their toes."

"If ever there was a time when the utmost vigilance is required," he concluded, "it is upon this voyage."

The day, despite its ominous reveille, was calm and uneventful. No periscope broke the surface of the sea and no aeroplanes were seen in the sky. The battleship tore through the seas at her usual high speed, with a destroyer ahead and, one on each beam.

Mr. Churchill, whose leg injury was rapidly responding to massage, was still in bed and had developed a slight cold. That evening he appeared at the film dressed, not in his blue mess uniform, but in the siren suit. It was commonly believed, but I never verified it, that the films that night, and during the remainder of the voyage, had been flown out to us by Lord Beaverbrook. One film that night was Donald Duck in *Foxhunting*, followed by Laurel and Hardy in *Saps at Sea*. The Surgeon-Commander, who sat next to me, was wondering all the time whether he should have kept the Prime Minister in bed. It was, therefore, a relief to him when Mr. Churchill rose at the end of the film and went straight to his cabin, remarking, as he left us, "a gay but inconsequent entertainment!"

The sea became wild on Thursday, August 14th, and the ship began to move as she had done on the outward voyage. The Map Room chart showed an interesting distribution of U-boats. It looked as though a pack of them were moving up to lie across our course; and at one time we were so near to them that we reduced speed to allow the destroyers to do a little scouting. They were unable to detect anything, and we were soon forging ahead again.

The Prime Minister was still in bed, his cold slightly better. It was said that the doctor had told Mr. Churchill that he was smoking too many cigars. Mr. Churchill replied that he had known that for years. The doctor then became firm and asked Mr. Churchill to promise to smoke no more cigars that day. Mr. Churchill bargained for just one, and the doctor reluctantly gave way.

Meanwhile the battleship continued to plough through the storm, her course set for Iceland, where we hoped to arrive on the morning of Saturday, August 16th. All those officers not on duty assembled in the wardroom to hear a broadcast by Mr. Attlee from London. Father Driscoll had been busily engaged an hour before the broadcast in driving out the devils and, wonderful to relate, the wireless seemed to be working well.

As the time drew near, every chair was occupied, and officers grouped themselves round the wireless eagerly waiting to learn what had happened at Placentia Bay. Although we had been there, we had no idea what had occurred. We had seen coming and going, and we had been aware of an atmosphere of urgency and importance, but not one word had been spoken by anyone concerned in the discussions. For all we knew, America might have decided to declare war. That was really what we hoped to hear.

Father Driscoll switched on the wireless, and, after an opening explosion, Mr. Attlee's voice filled the wardroom of the battleship. All over the world, I suppose, other people were listening, but we, and other similar groups in the battleship, were, I thought, probably the most interesting group of all—the *Prince of Wales* learning of the Atlantic Charter from London! How typical of modern civilisation.

Mr. Attlee began by saying that the President and the Prime Minister had met somewhere at sea, a remark which inspired loud cries of "No!" "We don't believe it!" and "Hear, hear!" Then we heard, point by point, the clauses of the Atlantic Charter. I have since been told that in clubs, and places where men gathered to hear the broadcast, faces grew long with disappointment as Mr. Attlee proceeded, and the exciting rumours, set about by Mr. Churchill's Atlantic journey were all deflated in an atmosphere of anti-climax. Curiously enough, precisely the same scene took place in the ward-room of the *Prince of Wales*. What we had all subconsciously hoped for, and not, perhaps, entirely subconsciously, was a declaration that America was coming into battle with us; the only thing that seemed to us to justify the dramatic encounter in the Atlantic between the two statesmen. In comparison with that, words, no matter how admirable, were a disappointment.

We sat looking at one another, remembering the launches going to and from the *Prince of Wales*, the staff meetings, the air of bustle and excitement; and this was all they meant! We were not, of course, statesmen. We knew nothing of the difficulties. Like all people at war, we had a pretty shrewd measure of our adversary, and we knew that, sooner or later, somehow, and in someway, America would come in with us and fight; then, we asked ourselves, why not now?

"Well," said a senior officer when the wireless had been switched off, "I expect there was far more to it than just that!"

And someone else suggested that the Council of Placentia was like one of those icebergs encountered in the Atlantic, the largest part of which remains invisible.

I remembered Mr. Churchill's words to me one night as he left the ship. "I have an idea that something really big may be happening—something really big." Perhaps the first thing necessary, I told myself, before two great nations can fight twice in one generation is to raise a Standard. It was George Washington who said: "Let us raise a standard to which the wise and honest can repair; the rest is in the hands of God."

Would ages to come, I wondered, see in the Atlantic Charter the raising of the Anglo-American Standard? We knew too little to be able to say yes or no.

That evening in my cabin I reflected upon the great event I had seen. I had discussed the drawing up of the Charter with someone who was there, and I learned from him with what passionate sincerity the two men responsible for it had composed their common principles, and with what consummate care they had put them down in words. The scene must have been a good one: the President's cabin aboard the *Augusta*, a fine room, as warships' cabins go, but still a cabin in a ship at sea; outside, the noise of picquet boats passing here and there, through the scuttle a circle of bare rock and, beneath the hard electric lights, the President of the United States and the Prime Minister of Great Britain sitting together in that small white room drawing up a new charter for Humanity; a splendid charter but one that, after all, was drawn up long ago upon a mountain side in Galilee.

The wording of the Charter, I gathered, is such a collaboration that it would be impossible now, so many times has the original draft been re-drawn, to discover which sentence might be traced to England and which to America, which to Churchill and which to Roosevelt. Just here and there, however, are gleams of both minds. When the first draft was read it ran as follows:

"The President of the United States and the Prime Minister, Mr. Churchill, representing His Majesty's Government in the United Kingdom, deem it right . . ."

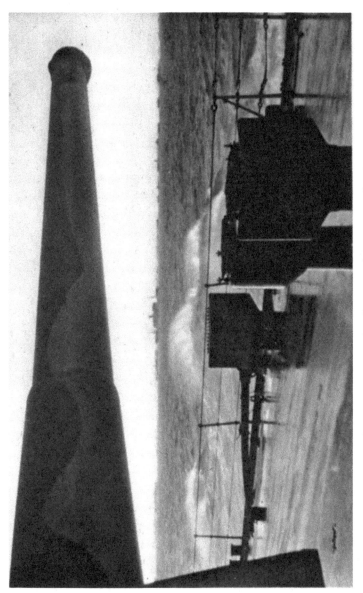

The convoy seen under the guns of the *Prince of Wales*

Mr. and Mrs. Churchill at King's Cross station on the Prime Minister's return from the Atlantic Meeting

The speaker was promptly interrupted by the voice of Mr. Churchill.

"*Being met together*, deem it right . . ." he said.

The script was altered and the speaker re-read it.

". . . representing His Majesty's Government in the United Kingdom, *being met together*, deem it right to make known certain common principles in the national policies of their respective countries on which they base their hopes for a better future for the world."

Then Clause Six is strongly reminiscent.

"After the final destruction of Nazi tyranny, they hope to see established a peace which will afford to all nations the means of dwelling in safety within their own boundaries, and which will afford assurance that all the men in all the lands may live out their lives *in freedom from fear and want*."

Freedom from fear and want! Did not President Roosevelt make a speech before Congress on January 6th, 1941, in the course of which he said:

"In future days we will look forward to the four essential human freedoms—freedom of speech and expression everywhere; the freedom of every person, and the right to worship God in their own way everywhere; *freedom from want; and freedom from fear*."

Again on May 4th, 1941, the President, when unveiling a national shrine to President Woodrow Wilson, used these words:

> "We will accept only a world consecrated to freedom of speech and expression and the freedom of every person to worship God in his own *way, freedom from want and freedom from terrorism.* Is such a world impossible of attainment?" he asked. "Magna Carta, the Declaration of Independence, the Constitution of the United States, the Emancipation Proclamation, and every other milestone of human progress, all were ideals which seemed impossible of attainment—yet they were attained."

So said the President in May; in August he set down his love of freedom in the Atlantic Charter in almost the same words. It was strange to think that in the solitude of that bay in Newfoundland an event as important to the future of Mankind as Magna Carta and the Declaration of Independence had been consummated while the little boats sped across the grey water and the low clouds settled upon the hills.

That night, for the first time, Mr. Churchill failed to appear after dinner. His temperature was slightly above normal, and the doctor had kept him, not without some difficulty, in bed.

We watched a film called *Power Dive*, finding it, without Mr. Churchill, like meat without salt. We realised that he had been the hero of all our films. Later that night I dropped into the Map Room on my way to bed to see what was happening. The U-boats were edging up in a rather uncomfortable way. We had altered course to avoid them during the afternoon and again at 6.30 p.m.

XIII

CONVOY

THE *Prince of Wales* was an unusual and threatening spectacle steaming at full speed with her destroyer screen, and should it have happened that some young man in command of a corvette, mistaking her for the *Deutschland*, had sent out a wireless yelp for assistance; well, someone might have been listening.

Therefore we had taken good care to avoid convoys. We did on one occasion sight two ships on the sky-line—my diary says it was on Friday, August 8th, during the outward voyage—but we rapidly altered course in order to remain invisible.

But all the time Mr. Churchill was longing to see a convoy. He used to go down to the Map Room time after time and measure the distance of the nearest, and so keen was his desire to see the life blood of Britain in circulation that the Captain and First Sea Lord knew that sooner or later his wish would have to be gratified. And this happened on Friday, August 15th.

There was a magnificent convoy of seventy-two ships ahead of us. They had, of course, been plotted on the map for some time and, as we rapidly overhauled them on Friday, Mr. Churchill, now restored to health, pointed out that only a slight deflection from our course would take us into them. It was therefore decided to do this, and a wireless warning to the corvettes was accordingly sent out.

The first I knew of it was when I met the signal officer in the ward-room during the afternoon. He was poring over a code book and seemed rather worried. He explained his problem.

"The signal I'm to make to the convoy," he said, "is 'The Prime Minister wishes you the best of luck.' But there's no signal for the Prime Minister in the International Code. The nearest thing is 'The Chief Minister of State,' which doesn't sound a bit right to me."

"Is there a flag for church?" I asked.

"Yes."

"And hill?"

"I see the idea—Churchill."

He came back later with the message changed to "Good Voyage, Churchill."

"I shall spell out Churchill," he said. "There can't be any mistake then."

It was not until eight-thirty that evening that we ran into the convoy. I was in the ward-room studying American magazine advertisements at the time. The telephone rang and George Ferguson spoke from the bridge, telling me to go out on the quarter-deck at once.

I ran out and saw an amazing sight. We were racing through the middle of the convoy. There were tramps, tankers, liners and whalers, salty old tubs and cargo boats of every type, age and size on each side of us, the nearest only two hundred yards away, the crews clustered on decks and fo'c'sles, waving their caps in the air and cheering like mad.

Never had I seen anything like it in my life. After days on a lonely ocean, to come into this fleet seventy-two ships travelling in long lines and covering many square miles of the Atlantic would have been exciting even in peace-time. It was like meeting a town at sea, Blackburn or Oldham, with all the chimneys smoking.

Now and again a siren tried to give us the V sign in Morse, but came to grief on the dots. Men in shirt sleeves, sailors, a few passengers, stood clustered wherever they could see us best, waving away, laughing and shouting at the top of their voices, but the wind carried their words from us. I expect it was, "Good old Winnie!"

Guarding this mighty fleet were eight little grey corvettes lifting on the swell, snapping round the flanks of the convoy like sheep-dogs, scurrying up in rear to hurry on a laggard, and dashing off into the open as if they had smelt the big bad wolf.

We went through with our destroyer screen at twenty-two knots. The convoy was doing eight. If they were thrilling to us, we must have been equally thrilling to them as we shot ahead with our painted guns levelled and twelve coloured flags and a pennant flying from our main foremast. The pennant at the lower yard showed that the signal was made in the International Code. A three-flag hoist above it read, PYU – – "Good Voyage," and a nine-flag hoist on the port side spelt Churchill.

As each ship read the message we could hear the sound of cheering as we came level with them, we could see skippers laughing inside wheel-houses, trying to wave with one hand and touch off the siren with the other; and upon our bridge Winston Churchill waving his hand in the air, making a V with the forefingers of his right hand, was cheering as madly as any of the men who were cheering him.

As he looked over the sea from the altitude of the bridge, he could see the whole convoy moving towards England. He saw it spread out for miles over the Atlantic, moving in six columns. He saw ships with aeroplanes tied to their decks, he saw cargo-boats wallowing to the plimsol line with food and munitions, liners deep in the water with every kind of war material and tankers heavy with petrol—a stupendous and heartening sight for the leader of an island at war.

Having passed through them, we turned and saw our white wake streaking backward, and we saw the ships tossing in the tidal wave of our wash. Then, to our surprise, the *Prince of Wales* with her destroyers began to describe a circle, and we raced back behind the convoy. Why? What had happened? This had happened. The Prime Minister insisted on seeing it all over again!

So on we came a second time, the bright message still at our masthead, our grey guns levelled; the sea curving in two white lines from our bows; and they saw in us the majesty of British sea power as we saw in them the gallantry of the Merchant Navy. It was a grand meeting on the high seas in war-time. I doubt if there has ever been a finer. It symbolised the two great forces which have made Britain and her Empire great and powerful in the world; the two forces we must thank when we eat our bread in freedom at this hour. As I watched those merchant ships so heavily loaded pass by, I wished that everyone at home in England could have seen them too. No one, seeing those brave ships loaded with help for us passing through the battlefield of the North Atlantic,

could ever again waste a crust of bread or think it smart to
scrounge a pint of petrol.

Again the cheers sounded as the *Prince of Wales* went past.
V flags were hoisted by tramps and tankers, the deep sirens
of liners and the shrill yelps of tramps sent out one dash and
three misguided dots into the air of evening; and, once again,
we saw the tiny cheering figures; on decks and fo'c'sles as we
raced across the grey sea on our way. And, looking back at
them with pride and gladness in our hearts, we saw the convoy fade in the growing dusk to black dots on the sky-line;
then they disappeared and there remained only a smudge of
smoke to tell that seventy-two ships were going home to
England.

Mr. Churchill watched them until the dusk and the distance hid them from view. "A delectable sight," he said.

XIV

ICELAND

EARLY in the morning we came to a noble land of wild mountains cut and seared with the marks of volcanic larva. It was the second fine day of our voyage and the only day of sunlight since the Sunday of the church parade.

Sunlight upon islands which do not experience much in the ordinary way has the effect of giving to them an extraordinary Cinderella brilliance, as if the land were anxious to show itself in brief, unusual splendour before the midnight of mists and rain sets in again. It was like that in Iceland on the morning of Saturday, August 16th, when we steamed into a long fiord upon a sea that might have washed the shore of Ithaca.

One had only to look at the scarred hills, the treeless sweeps of rock, the hard, cold moorlands and the mass of hill against lonely hill to think that such splendid summer days come perhaps rarely to that northern island.

Mr. Churchill was going to Reykjavík, the capital, to inspect troops and then to make a brief tour of the island. Some few weeks previously the United States had joined us in denying Iceland to the enemy by landing troops there, and by deciding to give naval escort to American convoys bound for Iceland. Describing that decision in the House of

Commons in July, Mr. Churchill had called it "one of the most important things that has happened since the war began." And now, straight from his meeting with the President, he was on his way to see the only land where British and American armed forces were working together.

Leaving the *Prince of Wales* at anchor in the fiord, we boarded a destroyer that was to carry us to the capital. Mr. Churchill, Sir John Dill, Sir Wilfrid Freeman, and handsome young Ensign Franklin D. Roosevelt were the principal members of the party. The destroyer steamed off down the beautiful fiord in the brilliant sunlight and, after rounding a headland, made for a distant line of coast where we could see a white town lying on the edge of the sea. It was exciting to watch that town grow nearer minute by minute, and to wonder what the capital of Iceland would be like.

Northern countries are, alas! a mystery to me. All my travels have been in Mediterranean lands. I knew, of course, that Iceland and Denmark were united under one king until Germany walked into Denmark in 1940, when the Icelanders severed the connection and elected their own Regent. I also knew that Iceland is one of the few countries in the world— may it not be the only one?—which does not maintain an army. But what the island was like, or what the Icelander is like, I had no idea at all. I should not have been surprised to encounter reindeer in the streets of Reykjavík, indeed, I half expected to do so. This, incidentally, is one of the rarest and sharpest of the joys of travel, this entry into the unknown. It is seldom in these days that the traveller visits a country which does not rent an office in Regent Street and whose beauties he had not already seen on glossy paper, whose pleasures and sporting possibilities he had not read of in persuasive pamphlets. I did, as a matter of fact, recollect one thing about Reykjavík, and it was perhaps a queer thing to remember: it was the starting-place of Jules Verne's romance, *A Journey to the Centre of the Earth*. What could have been more delightful than to be travelling towards a town of such memories?

We approached a small and busy seaport backed by wild hills and as innocent as a billiard-table of trees and even shrubs. From the sea, the houses looked small, neat and white. As the destroyer came slowly into harbour, we saw a naval, military and air force guard of honour drawn up on the dock, and behind them, in the road, at windows and tightly-packed upon all the ships in harbour, stood thousands of Icelanders. There was a tremendous roar of cheering as Mr. Churchill stepped ashore.

Having inspected the guard, he drove off in a car with the British Minister to make a call on the Regent, Sveinn Bjornsson. From the balcony of the Icelandic House of Parliament, Mr. Churchill, at the Regent's suggestion, addressed a large gathering and promised that during the war Britain and America would defend Iceland, and after the war would guarantee her independence. He then drove off to inspect the troops and to see the island.

Spring and I abandoned ourselves gladly to Reykjavík, which, after our prolonged incarceration aboard ship, looked to us a dazzling mixture of Paris and New York! We saw a small town—its population is forty thousand—evidently prosperous and busy, and quite unlike anything I had expected to see. Instead of frozen inhabitants driving reindeer or chewing blubber, we saw to our amazement, numbers of fashionable genuine ash blondes wearing an astonishing selection of hats. Perched upon those pale heads were hats as small as matchboxes and hats as large as archery targets, hats which might have been designed for a toy lancer and hats which were merely bits of cloth. And where did they come from? I had not the courage to ask, but if, like most things in the shops, they had come from England, what a surprising thing it is that we can make them and send them across the dangerous sea in war-time. I suppose that is what is known as maintaining our export trade.

War plays the strangest tricks upon us. In England now thousands of women go bare-legged, and admirable they look, but in Iceland, where, above all places, one might expect to see warm woollen stockings, every girl without exception wears silk. We came upon shops full of silk stockings, all made in England, and there were shop windows which displayed nothing else.

It is, of course, to be expected that in times when the entire productive capacity of a country is diverted to the making of war material, that the airs and graces of life should gradually peter out, as they have done in England. It is also to be expected that in an island which imports most of its food, and all of its luxuries, from overseas, war-time living should be plain. But in order to realise how far we have departed from pre-war days, how much in fact we are putting into the war, it is necessary to leave England and to come with surprise to places like Newfoundland and Iceland, neither of them the haunts of the pre-war hedonist, where money can still buy the unnecessary.

What was more impressive to us than shops in which one might buy pounds of butter, great cheeses, hams, tins of Icelandic caviare, pints of cream, chocolate and even photographic films, were the book-shops of Reykjavík. Their numbers and their varied contents would put to shame many an English town of twice or thrice Reykjavík's population. A remarkable feature was the high proportion of books in foreign languages, notably English and German. There was one window full of the latest English books, and these, I was told, are bought not by our own troops, but by the islanders.

Iceland must be the best educated and most intellectually curious country in the world, if the number of books published per head of the population is anything to go by. One book is published for every 466 inhabitants, which makes England appear illiterate with one book for every 3,205, and America positively cretinous with one book for every 12,497! But such statistics are not, fortunately, entirely satisfactory. What they do indicate, however, is that Iceland has an unusually developed hunger for the printed word, not only in Icelandic, but in other languages; and I was told that it is not unusual to meet farmers in remote parts who have taught themselves to speak and read both English and French. It may be that the dark winter evenings, when the sun is never seen and daylight is a brief affair, turns Iceland into a night-school.

It was interesting to walk about the streets watching the fashionable tow-haired girls, for whom there seemed no correspondingly fashionable male Icelanders, the British soldiers, the Americans, an occasional sailor, and the country folk still wearing old-fashioned clothes and what appeared to be the relics of a national costume.

We spoke to many of our soldiers, officers and men. There was an extraordinary division of opinion on the subject of life in Iceland. Some longed to be out of the island because they disliked it and because they felt they were out of the War, others were perfectly content and were worried only about friends and relatives at home. We came to the conclusion that their point of view largely depended upon their local contacts and social amenities. Some said that the Icelanders were charming; others that they regarded us as invaders and would have nothing to do with us. Some liked Reykjavík; others detested it and spoke affectionately of gun-posts in lonely corners of the island. With the assurance of day trippers, we chaffed these young men and told them they did not know how lucky they were to be living in an unblacked-out land of milk and honey.

In the course of our wanderings about Reykjavík, one shop above all others puzzled us. It was a florist's full of exotic hot-house blooms, notably carnations of superb quality. To see such evidence of horticulture in a land as bare as the Hebrides was so surprising that we went in and asked where the flowers were grown. We were told that, as Iceland is one of the most volcanic parts of the earth, springs of boiling water gush up all over the island, and it is this natural hot water laid on to glasshouses that makes it possible to cultivate flowers. Many houses in Reykjavík, and also a large swimming bath in the town get water piping hot from the earth by way of a pipe-line laid from springs about ten miles from the town.

When war broke out Iceland was in the middle of her most ambitious public work: the bringing of natural hot water into every house in the capital. The concrete bed for the pipe-line was laid and the pipes had been ordered in Denmark. When Germany occupied Denmark, she refused to allow the pipes out of the country; and so the scheme has been dropped until after the War.

We went to the Borg Hotel, which advertises itself as "the Palace of the North," and "the only modern hotel in Iceland"; there we encountered a cheerful gathering of officers from the ship, who had landed in a later launch. They were astonished as we were by the delights of Reykjavík, and each officer held a parcel containing silk stockings for wives and sweethearts at home. No one was absolutely certain he had bought the right size or colour, but no one doubted that his good intentions would be rapturously welcomed. The hotel was packed with a Saturday morning crowd of Icelanders, blonde ladies, British and American officers, and we had some difficulty in finding tables. Eventually they gave us cream soup and sea trout swimming in butter.

After lunch, Spring and I, accompanied by a British Intelligence Officer, motored for a little way into the island. It looked as I have seen the west coast of Ireland look on a sunny day: the sea bright blue, every cleft and valley in the mountains full of lavender shadows, and high gold clouds overhead. Long arms of the sea penetrated the land for great distances, running in between high hills, and there was a grand feeling of space and freedom. Far back in the interior, unfortunately invisible to us, was the famous volcano, Hecla, which we should dearly like to have seen. We were anxious also to visit the geyser which sends up a tower of hot water at intervals, and may even be persuaded to do it out of hours by a diet of soap-flakes; but this journey was impossible in the time at our disposal.

We came across several camps of Nissen huts surrounded by barbed wire and lying on bleak hill-sides with mountains behind. Two British sergeants came riding towards us on a couple of pot-bellied little Iceland ponies. They told us they always spent Saturday afternoons in the saddle.

Returning to Reykjavík, we reached the docks just in time to see Mr. Churchill arrive back from his tour. He appeared to be very happy, and behind him, looking oddly bridal, walked Inspector Thompson carrying an enormous bouquet of carnations. They were a gift to Mr. Churchill from the girls in the glass-houses.

The guard presented arms and Mr. Churchill and his party stepped aboard the destroyer, which immediately steamed off, taking us from the delectable isle. On the way back, General Dill discovered that some souvenir hunter had relieved his overcoat, which had been left in a car, of its gilt crossed batons. The thief was not a knowledgable collector, for he had taken a badge which he might have bought in the Army and Navy Stores for a few shillings while leaving behind the large gilt Royal cipher which only the Chief of the Imperial General Staff, Admirals of the Fleet, Field Marshals and A.D.C.'s to the King may wear.

The *Prince of Wales* sailed at eight-thirty in the evening and that night after dinner Mr. Churchill entertained us, and himself, to an American comedy called *Caught in the Draft*, which described the adventures of a young man who did not wish to join up.

XV

HOME AGAIN

I SUPPOSE our last day at sea, Sunday, August 17th, was probably the most hazardous of the voyage, though we saw no signs of either U-boat or bomber. The sea was, for one thing, admirably rough and the clouds were low. A U-boat was reported to be in our path and we made a detour to avoid it; others were reported not far away, and an air and destroyer patrol, which included our old friend, *Oribi*, were sent out from Scotland to deal with them.

There were two delightful farewell functions in the ship as we neared home. In the afternoon, the Prime Minister visited the Gun Room as the guest of the Midshipmen. He found himself surrounded by a number of alert and talkative young men, some of them mere boys, all of whom desired to know the most intimate secrets of the War Cabinet. Mr. Churchill was much amused by the questions put to him, although, of course, he was careful to treat every question seriously, parrying some of the most difficult with the skill of an old campaigner, and dealing faithfully, or as faithfully as he could, with each one. The young men were delighted and said he was a "wizard."

Much the same ordeal, perhaps even more severe, awaited him before dinner when he accepted an invitation to drink

a glass of sherry in the ward-room. Every officer in the ship
who was able to attend did so, bringing with him his favourite war problem. The Prime Minister stood in the centre of
a circle, firing answers to questions which even a hard-boiled
interviewer would have hesitated to put in war-time.

"Is Turkey coming into the War, sir?"

"What about the French Fleet, sir?"

"What did you make of Reynaud, sir?"

"Do you think America is coming in, sir?"

"What did the President say about . . .?"

"What are we going to do if . . .?"

And so on for nearly an hour. I thought the Prince
Minister was at his best in this wild cross-fire. With extraordinary skill, he replied to some questions without actually
answering them, but leaving the questioner with the happy
impression that he had been answered; which is not easy.
One young man demanded in a voice which would not be
denied.

"Tell us the true story of Hess, sir."

Mr. Churchill turned to him as if he were answering a
question in the House of Commons.

"The true story of Hess, sir," he replied, "is that a certain
gentleman thought he had only to come over here and put
a knot in the lion's tail and lead that noble creature back to
Germany. He was er—mistaken."

With the battleship plunging heavily through the seas,
we assembled that night to see William Powell and Myrna
Loy in *Love Crazy*, which we thought was Lord Beaverbrook's
best gift to us. It was also the last film we should see in those
extraordinary circumstances. We sat, as we had done so often,
in the trembling darkened room with the knowledge that

such an experience would never again fall to us. And when
Mr. Churchill turned and bowed to us and made his exit, we
felt the pang of parting which occurs in all voyages.

We awakened early on Monday, August 18th, because we
were to pass into Scapa Flow with our guns firing. The ship
was closed for action. All glass had been packed away. The
ward-room tumblers had been placed in shatter-proof boxes.
The glass doors of the book-case had been unscrewed and
put away. The scuttles were shut. Chairs and tables were
stacked on one another; and the ship steamed in an ominous
silence.

I went up on the bridge. Mr. Churchill and the Chiefs of
Staff were already there. Land was visible as a thin line on
the sky. The target was miles away to starboard and I could
not see it. Someone gave me a piece of cotton-wool and
advised me to plug my ears; and so I waited for the coming
explosion.

I heard a voice call "fire" down a speaking tube, and the
next moment it seemed that the ship had stopped, or had
been displaced to one side, as four tongues of hot light shot
from the forward fourteen-inch turret, followed by clouds
of white smoke and accompanied by a noise like the Day of
Judgment. I just had time to notice that the ship, unaffected
by that appalling explosion, was calmly steaming as usual
with a slight hiss of water against her sides, when it happened again, then a third time; and I seemed to feel the
inch-thick plate-glass of the bridge windows shudder in the
back blast. Then the other armaments joined in, including
the multiple pom-poms, which sent a rain of shells skyward
at released balloons and filled the air with puff balls. The

noise was deafening, and thrilling too, and, when the silence came again, land was nearer; and someone on the bridge said it was good shooting.

We watched the hills take shape round Scapa, and we steamed majestically to our anchorage. An admiral came aboard. Men in other ships looked at us through telescopes. Mr. Churchill, standing before a microphone, spoke to the ship's company ranked row on blue row. He told them of the historic occasion in which they had played a part and he spoke of the great cause they serve. The sound of their voices echoed among the hills as, with caps off, they cheered and cheered again. And Winston Churchill smiled at them under the peak of his blue cap and brought out a cigar.

Our last destroyer waited with steam up to take us to the mainland of Scotland. In a little while we saw the half-circle of shore which had wept so bitterly at our departure fourteen days previously. In Thurso stood the Prime Minister's beautiful train, as if it had never moved, and there was the same genial man in brown who came up and, greeting me by name, hoped we had had a pleasant trip, as if we had been sun-bathing in Florida.

In the morning Mr. Churchill stepped out at King's Cross and kissed his wife; in the background stood the members of the Cabinet.

Six days later the world heard him describe the meeting at Placentia Bay.

"This was a meeting," he said, "which marks for ever in the pages of history the taking up by the English-speaking nations amid all this peril, tumult and confusion, of the guidance of the fortunes of the broad, toiling masses in all the continents, and our loyal effort, without any clog of self-ish interest, to lead them forward out of the miseries into which they have been plunged back to the broad high-road of freedom and justice. This is the highest honour and the most glorious opportunity which could ever have come to any branch of the human race."

NOTE

The text of the Atlantic Charter as first published in London and Washington differed by the omission from the British text of three words, due to transmission by telegraph. These words printed within brackets in the following text have now been added to the final British version as printed in the Treaty Series (No. 5 of 1942) and issued on September 2nd, 1942.

APPENDIX

A.—THE ATLANTIC CHARTER.

B.—MR. CHURCHILL'S DESCRIPTION OF THE ATLANTIC MEETING (*August 24th*, 1941).

C.—LIST OF OFFICERS, H.M.S. "PRINCE OF WALES" (*August,* 1941).

A.—THE ATLANTIC CHARTER

THE PRESIDENT of the United States (of America) and the Prime Minister, Mr. Churchill, representing His Majesty's Government in the United Kingdom, being met together, deem it right to make known certain common principles in the national policies of their respective countries on which they base their hopes for a better future for the world.

FIRST, their countries seek no aggrandisement, territorial or other.

SECOND, they desire to see no territorial changes that do not accord with the freely expressed wishes of the people concerned.

THIRD, they respect the right of all peoples to choose the form of government under which they will live; and they wish to see sovereign rights and self-government restored to those who have been forcibly deprived of them.

FOURTH, they will endeavour, with due respect for their existing obligations, to further enjoyment of all States, great or small, victor or vanquished, of access, on equal terms, to the trade and to the raw materials of the world which are needed for their economic prosperity.

FIFTH, they desire to bring about the fullest collaboration between all nations in the economic field, with the object of securing for all improved labour standards, economic advancement, and social security.

SIXTH, after the final destruction of (the) Nazi tyranny, they hope to see established a peace which will afford to all nations the means of dwelling in safety within their own boundaries, and which will afford assurance that all the men in all the lands may live out their lives in freedom from fear and want.

SEVENTH, such a peace should enable all men to traverse the high seas and oceans without hindrance.

EIGHTH, they believe (that) all of the nations of the world, for realistic as well as spiritual reasons, must come to the abandonment of the use of force. Since no future peace can be maintained if land, sea or air armaments continue to be employed by nations which threaten, or may threaten, aggression outside of their frontiers, they believe, pending the establishment of a wider and permanent system of general security, that the disarmament of such nations is essential. They will likewise aid and encourage all other practicable measures which will lighten for peace-loving peoples the crushing burden of armaments.

The Atlantic Charter was accepted and endorsed by the representatives of Belgium, Czechoslovakia, Greece, Luxemburg, the Netherlands, Norway, Poland, U.S.S.R., Yugoslavia and Free France at a meeting of the Inter-Allied Council held at St. James's Palace on September 29th 1941.

B.—Mr. CHURCHILL'S DESCRIPTION OF THE ATLANTIC MEETING
(August 24th, 1941)

On Sunday, August 24th, 1941, six days after his return home, Mr. Churchill made the following broadcast*:

"I thought you would like me to tell you something about the voyage I made across the ocean to meet our great friend, the President of the United States. Exactly where we met is a secret, but I don't think I shall be indiscreet if I go so far as to say that it was 'somewhere in the Atlantic.'

"In a spacious landlocked bay which reminded me of the west coast of Scotland, powerful American warships protected by strong flotillas and far-ranging aircraft, awaited our arrival, and, as it were, stretched out a hand to help us in. Our party

*Reprinted from *The Unrelenting Struggle* by courtesy of Mr. Winston Churchill and Messrs. Cassell & Co., Ltd.

arrived in the newest, or almost the newest, British battleship, the *Prince of Wales*, with a modest escort of British and Canadian destroyers.

"There for three days I spent my time in company, and I think I may say in comradeship, with Mr. Roosevelt, while all the time the chiefs of staff and naval and military commanders, both of the British Empire and the United States, sat together in continual council.

"President Roosevelt is the thrice-chosen head of the most powerful State and community in the world. I am the servant of King and Parliament at present charged with the principal direction of our affairs in these fateful times, and it is my duty also to make sure, as I have made sure, that anything I say or do in the exercise of my office is approved and sustained by the whole British Commonwealth of Nations.

"Therefore this meeting was bound to be important because of the enormous forces at present only partially mobilised but steadily mobilising, which are at the disposal of these two major groupings of the human family, the British Empire and the United States, who, fortunately for the progress of mankind, happen to speak the same language and very largely think the same thoughts, or anyhow think a lot of the same thoughts. The meeting was therefore symbolic. That is its prime importance. It symbolises in a form and manner which everyone can understand in every land and every clime, the deep underlying unities which stir and, at decisive moments, rule the English-speaking peoples throughout the world. Would it be presumptuous for me to

say that it symbolises something even more majestic, namely
the marshalling of the good forces of the world against the
evil forces which are now so formidable and triumphant,
and have cast their cruel spell over the whole of Europe and
a large part of Asia? This was a meeting which marks for
ever in the pages of history the taking up of the English-
speaking nations amid all this peril, tumult and confusion,
of the guidance of the fortunes of the broad toiling masses
in all the continents, and our loyal effort, without any clog
of selfish interest, to lead them forward out of the miseries
into which they have been plunged back to the broad high-
road of freedom and justice. This is the highest honour and
the most glorious opportunity which could ever have come
to any branch of the human race."

Mr. Churchill went on to describe the German attack on
Russia and America's attempts to reach a settlement with
the Japanese. Then he returned to the Atlantic meeting:

"We had the idea when we met there, the President and I,
that without attempting to draw final and formal peace aims
or war aims, it was necessary to give all peoples, and especially the oppressed and conquered peoples, a simple, rough
and ready wartime statement of the goal towards which the
British Commonwealth and the United States mean to
make their way, and thus make a way for others to march
with them upon a road which will certainly be painful and
may be long. There are, however, two distinct and marked
differences in this joint declaration from the attitude adopted
by the Allies during the latter part of the last war, and no
one should overlook them.

The United States and Great Britain do not now assume that there will never be any more war again. On the contrary, we intend to take ample precautions to prevent its renewal in any period we can foresee by effectually disarming the guilty nations while remaining suitably protected ourselves.

"The second difference is this: That instead of trying to ruin German trade by all kinds of additional trade barriers and hindrances, as was the mood of 1917, we have definitely adopted the view that it is not in the interests of the world and of our two countries that any large nation should be unprosperous or shut out from the means of making a decent living for itself and its people by its industry and enterprise."

Mr. Churchill again turned to the international situation, and concluded with a description of the church parade aboard the *Prince of Wales*:

"We had a Church Parade on the Sunday in our Atlantic bay. The President came on the quarterdeck of the *Prince of Wales,* where there were mingled together many hundreds of American and British sailors and marines. The sun shone bright and warm, while we all sang the old hymns which are our common inheritance, and which we learned as children in our homes. We sang the hymn founded on the psalm which John Hampden[5]s soldiers sang when they bore his body to the grave, and in which the brief precarious span of human life is contrasted with the immutability of Him to whom a thousand ages are but as yesterday when it is past and as a watch in the night.

"We sang the sailors' hymn 'For those'—and there are very many—'in peril on the sea.' We sang 'Onward Christian Soldiers,' and indeed, I felt that this was no vain presumption but that we had the right to feel that we were serving a cause for the sake of which a trumpet has sounded from on high. When I looked upon that densely-packed congregation of fighting men of the same language, of the same faith, of the same fundamental laws, of the same ideals, and now to a large extent of the same interests, and certainly in different degrees facing the same dangers, it swept across me that here was the only hope, but also the sure hope, of saving the world from measureless degradation. And so we came back across the ocean waves, uplifted in spirit, fortified in resolve."

C.—H.M.S. "PRINCE OF WALES"—LIST OF OFFICERS
(*August,* 1941)

Captain J. C. Leach, M.V.O.

Commander H. F. Lawson.
Commander (E) L. J. Goudy.
Paymaster Commander A. J. Wheeler.
Surgeon Commander F. B. Quinn.

The Reverend W. J. Driscoll, R.C. Chaplain.
The Reverend W. G. Parker, Chaplain.

Lieutenant Commander A. G. Skipwith.
Lieutenant Commander (T) R. F. Harland.
Lieutenant Commander (G) C. W. McMullem.

Lieutenant Commander (N) G. W. ROWELL.
Lieutenant Commander C. G. LAWSON.
Lieutenant Commander A. H. TERRY.

Lieutenant Commander R. S. CASEMENT.
Acting Lieutenant Commander G. C. I. FERGUSON, R.N.V.R.
Lieutenant (P) C. R. BATEMAN.
Lieutenant (G) R. G. BECKWITH.
Lieutenant (Q) J. W. COLLETT.
Lieutenant I. D. S. FORBES.
Lieutenant E. V. DAWSON, R.N.V.R.
Lieutenant M. A. BUXTON, R.N.V.R.

Lieutenant Commander (E) R. O. LOCKLEY.
Lieutenant (E) A. J. CAWTHRA.
Lieutenant (E) D. E. H. WILDISH.
Lieutenant (E) P. J. A. SLADE.
Lieutenant (E) J. E. DYER-SMITH.
Lieutenant (E) C. W. HODGESON.
Lieutenant (E) F. T. HEALY.

Captain C. D. L. AYLWIN, R.M.

Lieutenant G. T. B. SHERIDAN, R.M.
Lieutenant C. G. VERDON, R.M.

Instr. Lieutenant T. W. SMITH.
Ord. Lieutenant E. LANCASTER.

Surgeon Lieutenant Commander E. D. CALDWELL.
Surgeon Lieutenant A. C. FRANKS.

Surgeon Lieutenant (D) R. D. JOHNSTON.

Paymaster Lieutenant Commander M. A. MCMULLEN.
Paymaster Lieutenant W. T. BLUNT.

Sub Lieutenant E. J. KEMPSON, R.N.V.R.
Sub Lieutenant G. A. G. BROOKE.
Sub Lieutenant J. B. WOMERSLY.
Sub Lieutenant R. C. RIPLEY, R.N.V.R.
Sub Lieutenant A. G. FRANKLIN, R.N.V.R.
Sub Lieutenant G. H. HOPKINSON, R.N.V.R.
Sub Lieutenant (A) P. D. LLOYD.
Sub Lieutenant (Sp) R. H. PETERS, R.N.V.R.
Sub Lieutenant (Sp) S. E. PADDON, R.C.N.V.R.
Sub Lieutenant (Sp) A. G. TEMPLE-CARRINGTON.

Paymaster Sub Lieutenant J. G. BASKCOMB, R.N.R.
Mr. F. LUXTON, Commissioned Gunner.
Mr. C. G. A. MURPHY, Commissioned Gunner.
Mr. L. H. JACKSON, Commissioned Gunner (T).
Mr. T. E. MURCH, Commissioned Shipwright.
Mr. R. SATCHWILL, Commissioned Telegraphist.
Mr. H. S. JARRETT, Commissioned Engineer.
Mr. M. J. CUMMINS, Schoolmaster (CWO).
Mr. E. H. MARCHANT, Commissioned Electrician.
Mr. H. W. S. REED, Commissioned Supply Officer.
Mr. H. J. EVANS, Gunner.
Mr. J. WHITE, Gunner.
Mr. H. B. SPILLER, Bosun.
Mr. G. T. FISHER, Signal Bosun.
Mr. E. J. BOFFEY, Warrant Engineer.

Mr. W. WINCHESTER, Warrant Mechanician.

Midshipman C. P. ALLEN, R.I.N.
Midshipman K. H. F. CLARK.
Midshipman W. F. B. FAULKNER.
Midshipman D. G. ROOME.
Midshipman A. W. TRIBE.
Midshipman R. H. LEIR, R.C.N.
Temporary Midshipman P. S. EVANS, R.N.R.
Temporary Midshipman P. A. B. HUNT, R.N.R.
Temporary Midshipman M. H.R. PRUETT, R.N.R.
Temporary Midshipman W. W. ROBINSON, R.N.R.
Temporary Midshipman J. H. P. SLY, R.N.R.

Paymaster Midshipman M. HAY.
Paymaster Midshipman A. W. HEMSTEAD.
Paymaster Midshipman J. L. G. WATSON.

INDEX